DARK INTIMACY

Hope for Those in Difficult Prayer-Experiences

David J. Hassel, S.J.

Paulist Press
New York/Mahwah

The Publisher gratefully acknowledges the use of the poem, "A Creation Canticle," by Joseph Awad, reprinted by permission of the author.

INPRIMI POTEST
Robert A. Wild, S.J.
Provincial, Chicago Province of the Society of Jesus

Scripture quotations in this book are from the *New American Bible.*

Library of Congress Cataloging-in-Publication Data

Hassel, David J.
    Dark Intimacy

    Bibliography: p.
    1. Prayer. 2. Intimacy (Psychology)—Religious aspects—
Christianity. I. Title.
BV210.2.H366   1986   248.3'2   86–15061
ISBN 0-8091-2818-7 (pbk.)

Published by Paulist Press
997 Macarthur Blvd.
Mahwah, N.J. 07430

Printed and bound in the
United States of America

Contents

Dedicated
to

James J. Doyle, S.J.

Mentor Become Friend

Preface

People who talk much about intimacy in their lives usually do not have it. So, to write a book about intimacy in prayer is embarrassingly revealing. Yet prayer is intimacy, the deepest and most lasting of all intimacies. Consequently, something must be said about it—if only because the "instant intimacy" portrayed in the communication media is often shallow and misleading.

But there are other and better reasons for discussing the intimacy of prayer. For example, a person can overlook the signals of intimacy offered by Christ in prayer unless they are called to his or her attention. For these signals are naturally delicate since the Lord does not wish to frighten us or to lessen our freedom or to do any violence to us. Further, there are stages of intimacy and, as one enters a new stage where there may be new signals, one can falsely judge that intimacy has been lost.

It should be noted, also, that the intimacy enjoyed with a friend sharpens one's perception and appreciation of divine intimacy and vice versa. Here one witnesses the compenetration of the first and the second of the great commandments. "As often as you did it for one of my least brothers, you did it for me" (Mt 25:40). Indeed, the signals of intimacy in prayer reveal the qualities of that love which our God is. And one's way of receiving these signals shows the strengths and weaknesses of one's praying.

As you read along through the following chapters, it may suddenly strike you: "This book is talking about prayerful attitudes more than about specific ways of praying." And your judgment will be accurate. For, it seems to me, the root of all praying is a set of prayerful attitudes such as hunger for intimacy with God, gratitude for God's forgiveness of sins, strong hope in God amid one's sinfulness, eager desire to

1

serve God's people, sense of total dependence on God, empathy for persons-God-universe, appreciation for friendship with God and his people. Such prayerful attitudes are being mapped in this book because no action, no prayer escapes their pervasive influence. They make actual the Lord's seemingly impossible command "to pray always". However, they do atrophy if they are not actuated by decisive action for others and by specific ways of praying. At the same time, though, without them our decisions and prayer become listless.

These attitudes, of course, are sometimes implanted and at other times invigorated by the various sacraments. For example, baptism lifts our decisions and prayer into the Trinitarian life and confirmation encourages and focuses our service of God's people. Sacramental life, then, enriches prayer beyond our expectations—if our daily prayer of intimacy has taken us beyond impersonal routines into face-to-face and heart-to-heart meetings with the Lord. This is why the understanding of prayer as intimacy and the sacraments as intimate life-events has been emphasized in these following chapters.[1]

It is clear, then, why this book has intimacy in its title. Later, as one descends into the deeper stages of intimacy and its prayer, it will become more evident why the title is *Dark Intimacy*. Intimacy makes terrible demands on all partners in love, work and prayer. We have reason to be fearful of it even as we pursue it with all our mind, heart and will. For, in a moment, intimacy can move from tender peace to devastating cyclone, from desert experience to jungle feeling, from bright day to dark night. Indeed, the sacraments out of which prayer of intimacy rises are meant to illuminate and strengthen us in each major crisis and joy of life. It is hoped that this book will sketch a realistic approach to the beautiful, but dark, intimacy offered us by God in our daily praying.

Of course, little or nothing of this book would have appeared if it had not been for the trust and honesty of directees as they struggled in prayer of intimacy. Literally, they are the experience out of which this book rises. They are also the inspiration which brought this book to publication. For not rarely they had suffered guilt about their prayer when, as a matter of fact, they were praying (heroically, at times) at a new stage of intimacy. Relieving such guilt became important for me and spurred me to write this book. So, my gratitude to them is great.

But I am particularly indebted to the late James J. Doyle, S.J., emeritus professor of theology at Loyola University of Chicago, who guided me carefully through this book. Mary Anne Hoope, B.V.M., associate professor of theology and director of undergraduate theology at Mundelein College of Chicago, improved greatly the whole manuscript with her extensive critique. Dr. Julia Lane, dean of Loyola University's school of nursing, patiently and encouragingly read an early version of the manuscript. A number of Jesuits worked with me on individual chapters; their names are given in gratitude within the first footnote of each chapter.

If the Jesuit community at Loyola University of Chicago had not supported me during an unpaid sabbatical, this book could not have been started; their support, of course, was much more than economic. And if the Cenacle Sisters of Chicago and Warrenville had not offered me three opportunities to test out these chapters on themselves and their retreatants, I would not have had the benefit of encouraging critiques and significant additions to my thought. As always, the author does not get very far without a skillful editor doing hidden work; in this instance it is Donald F. Brophy.

Finally I would like to thank Sr. Mary Anthony Wagner, O.S.B., editor of *Sisters Today,* and Kenneth Baker, S.J., editor of the *Homiletic and Pastoral Review,* for publishing articles and then releasing them to be included as chapters of this book. Daniel F.X. Meenan, S.J., editor of the *Review for Religious,* not only allowed me to get early critique of two chapters by publishing them first as articles but also made valuable suggestions for improving them. To all three editors I am deeply grateful.

Stage One
The Hunger-Fear Paradox of Intimacy:
"Go Away Closer!"[1]

Intimacy is the key word in current spiritual literature. So many books and articles sport the title that one could mistakenly think that intimacy is well understood and practiced. There is nothing we humans crave more, fear more, and fumble more than intimacy. The adolescent peers deeply within the self: "Will anyone ever care for me, really care for me—and what do I do when someone does care for me?" The young engaged couple wonders at times: "Will our love eventually evaporate or will it grow so intense that it will overwhelm us with its demands?" Indeed the mystics have an ambivalent craving for intimacy that astounds even them; for they know that at times intimacy with God hurts terribly while at other times it is the most rewarding among all human joys. Yes, we have all met the person whose every action seems to say: "Go away closer!" This person invites you to the door of his or her heart and then slams it shut whenever you start to enter. Have we not all slammed doors suddenly in panic and then wondered why?

1. Ambiguous Occasions of Intimacy

Not a few imitations of intimacy mislead and cruelly dash our hopes against the rocks of reality. Everyone somewhere along the line has had a four-hour conversation with an engaging seat-partner on a coast-to-coast flight, a conversation in which both say much more than they had intended about their private lives so that they are embarrassed to meet again—even at the baggage counter. Does anybody pass the so-called intimate bar without fantasizing: "Is there someone inside who, in the quiet atmosphere of a relaxing drink, would

5

eventually become a close friend?'' The ship-cruise
advertisement plays on our psychic hungers: ''Make friends in
the family intimacy of a Caribbean cruise on the 250
passenger Dutch liner: Future Hope.'' Then there is the
person who warmly invites intimate conversation and, if one
takes the bait, is found to be a busy scandal-monger or a
friendly scalp-hunter (''Yes, I know him well; we've had some
heavy conversations together'').

Even situations meant for intimacy may yield only
frustration. After a thirty-five year marriage the wife can say:
''He never confides in me and never will, I guess.'' And her
husband may on another occasion remark: ''She simply cannot
comprehend my worries, my interests, my hopes.'' The young
religious expecting instant brotherhood or sisterhood in the
community may find the novitiate a place of isolation and
superficial exchange. There is also the favorite brother who
returns home after a five-year tour at the U.S.A. Budapest
embassy and seems unable to share with his sister the reasons
for the large changes which she notices in him: restlessness,
secret anger, inability to laugh at small family jokes. Often
enough, then, one's craving for intimacy is only intensified,
not satisfied, by situations promising intimacy.

2. Signs and Conditions for Intimacy

One can give definitions of intimacy such as the sharing of
one's deepest joys, sorrows, ambitions, fears, loves and hopes
with someone admired, trusted, and faithful. But such
definitions mean less than the signs by which we recognize
intimacy: the reverent kiss in a moment of good fortune, the
reassuring hug in time of distress, the smile of deep
satisfaction in the other's presence, the wink of warm
affection across a crowded cocktail party, the secret and crazy
language arising out of a shared lifetime, the sigh of longing
and the slow murmuring of the beloved's name, the air of
expectancy and lightheartedness when the friend is about to
arrive at the airport gate.

Yet signs are not enough to reveal what intimacy is. We need to look behind these manifestations to the conditions which cause them. For instance, for what does a person search when wanting to confide in someone? Does not the confider first seek someone who, absorbed and undistracted, listens intently without interrupting one's long story? One also needs to find integrity; the confidant would never betray a divulged secret, would be fully honest in his or her reactions, would not be suddenly scandalized at one's revelations but is actually shock-proof. One also expects the confidant to resonate to one's feelings, to be alert to the needs of the confider and even occasionally to share his or her own secret feelings and hopes (so that there is some mutual give and take). It would also be good if the confidant were capable of playfulness and humor and were not fearful of occasionally acting the fool. Lastly, the confider expects of the confidant prudent advice arising out of much personal experience and out of close knowledge of and feeling for what the confider has described.

Here we have a number of conditions which enable intimacy to happen if the confider and the confidant can hold the conversation together with a willing endurance of each other's shortcomings. These very conditions for intimate exchange provide a profile of the perfect confidant. They might almost be a picture of Christ himself operating in our experience.

3. Prayer Is Intimacy at Eight Ever-Deeper Stages

But how does all this talk about ambiguous occasions, expressions, and conditions for intimacy apply to prayer? They apply neatly because prayer is intimacy at its best. In God we have a confidant always ready for the occasion of sharing deeply his and our life, a confidant who gives delicate and strong expressions of intimacy within us and who fulfills easily all the conditions for intimacy just described. The proof of these statements could be one's own experience of eight types of prayer, each of which corresponds to ever deeper

stages of intimacy with God and each of which is rooted
within the experience of a particular sacrament. For each type
of prayer and each corresponding sacrament is meant to be a
deeper discovery of God within a peak- or valley-event of
one's life. Let us describe briefly these eight types of prayer.

The first type is simply the awareness of a deep hunger
for intimacy which may be directed to another human but
implicitly includes God. This hunger is itself prayer so long as
God is not excluded from it. If the reader, while noting the
previously described ambiguities, signs and conditions of
intimacy, felt the stirrings of desire for intimacy with others
and with God, this movement was itself the beginning of
prayer.

At a deeper second stage occurs the prayer of day-to-day
intimacy. It arises out of life's daily events starting even
before we were born. For we have been created by the
intimacy of intercourse, of gestation in the womb, and of
constant attendance, protection and nourishment during the
infant years. Thus each human being is made to be intimate
from the first moments of zygotic life. After one's infancy, this
sense of intimacy grows with language learning, with tight
interdependence of family living, with long-term schooling,
with teamwork of sports and work, and with shared joy at
success and sorrow at failure. In fact, each human being grows
ever more hungry for intimacy because each is created for the
crowning intimacy within the life of the Triune God. Thus
these conditions for prayer of day-to-day intimacy form the
second stage of intimate prayer. They are the basis for
companioning Christ daily.

On this score, the prayer of daily intimacy is basic to a
healthy spiritual life. In this second type or stage of intimate
prayer a person faces God one-to-one in nakedness without
being able to hide behind someone else's praying.[2] It takes
God off the shelf and puts him into one's heart, mind, and
daily actions. Since this radical experience sustains all the
other types of prayer to be profiled below, it draws heavily
upon the sacrament of baptism or rebirth and upon the
companioning Gospel-life of Christ, the intimate friend. It is

the taproot of all prayer deep in the loam of the conditions for intimacy. Without this day-to-day prayer of intimacy, all other types or stages of prayer gradually dry up and die out.

A third type of prayer of intimacy is the prayer of forgiveness. Only those dearest to us can hurt us deeply not only before their forgiveness, but more so during and after forgiveness. To forgive is not to forget the hurt; it is to remember it without recrimination, bitterness and revenge. It is to strangely treasure the offender and even to forgive oneself so that God can be felt forgiving the forgiver. Naturally, this prayer is rooted in the sacrament of reconciliation and looks to the vulnerability of Christ in the Gospels (cf. Lk 6:27–38: "Be compassionate as your Father is compassionate"; Lk 15:1ff.—the mercy parables). Since this prayer requires mature reflection on one's life-needs and operates where despair could take over, it is also rooted in the sacrament of confirmation.

A fourth type of prayer of intimacy, that of admitted sinfulness, enters into an even deeper intimacy than the previous prayer of forgiveness. For it involves the rather horrifying experience of recognizing one's capacity to commit any sin imaginable and of seeing how one's sins sap all intimacy with others, God and self. Still, the acceptance of these two bitter facts about oneself frees one to use personal weaknesses and past sins to praise God. For here the praying person admits total dependence on a rescuing God of marvelous mercy and thus feels ultimate gratitude for God's faithfulness. This prayer is also founded in the sacrament of reconciliation, but finds its nourishment in the pervasive covenant theme of the Old and New Testaments: God faithfully offers his friendship even amid human betrayal.

When the four previous prayer-types are sharply present in the praying person's experience, a fifth stage of intimacy opens up. It is the intimate "more" of apostolic work and prayer. This "more" is the unexpectedly fruitful results occurring both in one's work and in one's prayer. As one discovers, enjoys and praises this new presence, one finds care-ridden ambition to succeed at any cost diminishing. One gradually stops seeking total control over others, self, and the work situation. One is discovering the truly lasting values of life as if through the eyes of the sick. Not surprisingly, this prayer of the intimate apostolic "more" finds its life in the sacraments of confirmation and of the sick. Its growing strength and inventiveness come from prayerfully following, step by step, Christ's Gospel-training of the apostles.

A sixth deeper stage of intimacy is reached in the prayer of powerlessness. Here one discovers and reverences God's intimate mediation between spouses, friends, and vowed religious; and here one recognizes that God works most powerfully through one's weaknesses when one is administering to others. For nothing is more out of one's control, more difficult, more revealing of one's inadequacies (and yet more worthwhile) than marriage, friendship, and religious community. Prayer of powerlessness, however, is not mere confusion or malaise. Rather it contains a stark clarity about one's long-experienced inability to carry out cherished desires to serve and to love others and it reaffirms the conviction that, without God's continual assistance, one is inevitably doomed to failure.

It is, strange to say, a prayer of tranquillity set deep in the sacrament of marriage and in the quasi-sacraments of religous vows and of loyal, long-term friendship. Here God is recognized as our inmost strength and wisdom. Food for this prayer is found in the suffering-servant motif, in the biblical personages of Mary and John the Baptist, and in the beatitudes for the anawim, the marginal people. At this stage spiritual direction becomes almost a necessity.

At the seventh stage of intimacy one finds the *prayer of being.* It is characterized by a sweet bitterness, a full emptiness, and a bright darkness. Despite its being a union with God and with others, it seems to deny all intimacy precisely because of its depth and simplicity. But its discipline liberates one from manipulating others, from instructing God what to do next, from easy self-delusion, and from self-vaunting. Instead, it transforms one into a being-for-others, an imaging of Yahweh. Consequently, it is a homing prayer at the center of one's being—a homing to God, self, and community. Its source of strength not to manipulate others is the priesthood of the faithful and the sacrament of orders; its nourishment in prayer is the last supper, passion and death of Jesus.

The prayer of ultimate union occurs at the eighth and deepest stage of intimacy with God and others. It is precisely the compenetration of persons in their very beings, a compenetration supremely modeled in the Trinity of divine persons and fully consummated in the communion of saints. But it starts here in married family life, in friendships and in religious vowed life. For amid the awkwardnesses, the mistakes, the humorous shortcomings and the zany events of everyday routines, one has learned to accept the other as a totality, loving the other's goodness and not letting the other's evil interfere with one's love. One discovers within oneself an eternal patience with self and others, a confident peace, and a mysterious exuberance ready to do things great and small.

This prayer of ultimate union seems to sum up all the other types of prayer much as the Eucharist sums up and roots all the other sacraments in itself. It is the prayer of the Gospel resurrection-narrative, of the Acts of the Apostles, and of the Pauline contemplations in his Letters to the Ephesians and Colossians. Obviously, this eighth type of prayer is the core of liturgical prayer since the eight steps of deepening presence in the Eucharistic sacrifice lead down the eight stages of prayer of intimacy to the prayer of ultimate union.[3] Basically, prayer of ultimate union is the Ignatian "contemplation to attain divine love" now lived in a powerful passivity which energizes all one's actions.

4. Radical Prayer of Intimacy

This quick survey of eight types of intimacy-prayer (each of them occurring at a deeper stage of human experience and each of them finding its source in particular sacraments) is meant merely to stress the central factor of all prayer: the absolute need for face-to-face, one-to-one meeting with the

Lord at all stages of our being and our life. It also indicates
that without the first and second stages of intimacy-prayer
(the hunger for intimacy and the daily fifteen or thirty or sixty
minutes of one-to-one prayer with Christ), there is no taproot
to nourish the other six types or stages of this prayer into
steady growth. Nothing can be more discouraging for a
spiritual director than to find the good directee unable to set
aside time for this radical prayer of intimacy without which all
prayer, private and liturgical, begins to wither. Nothing
encourages the director more than to meet the directee who
is willing to gamble all other activities for the sake of this
privileged time alone with the Lord Jesus.

Nevertheless the slightly aware director has often heard
his or her inner self saying to the Lord: "Please, go away
closer," just as Peter did after the miraculous netting of fish
(Lk 5:8–9). Perhaps this personally experienced weakness will
enable the director to gracefully touch the directee's heart
and strengthen it for the prayer of daily intimacy.

At any rate, if one is experiencing some hunger for
intimacy at the first stage and if the deepening implications of
this hunger are vaguely felt, it may be time now to explore
carefully the remaining seven stages of prayer of intimacy.

Stage Two
Day-to-Day Prayer of Intimacy:
Root of All Other Prayer[1]

Despite our fear of intimacy, we have been created by intimacy, we continue to be fostered through intimacy, and we are destined for the fullest possible intimacy after death. Because intimacy is, therefore, the source of our very being and of our growth into full womanhood and manhood, it is the taproot of all prayer. Such statements as these demand some reflection on our life-experience. How can one say that a person is literally constituted by, through, and for intimacy?

1. We Are Created by, through, and for Intimacy

That we are created by intimacy is evident from the fact that our existence comes from the most intimate of all physical acts: intercourse. Further, the husband and wife's previous psychological and spiritual intimacy prepared and suffused this physical act. That was why the engagement period was so vital and beautiful for them. For, of its very nature, intercourse requires the blending of their minds and hearts as its psychological dimension and the embracing of their mutual trust as its spiritual dimension.

Then the embryonic child takes shape within the mother's womb by following the genetic gifts of father and mother, by sharing the mother's food and blood, by living in the mother's moods and deepest feelings, and by undergoing her sense of security or despair, elation or depression. The leap of John the Baptist in the womb of Elizabeth came with the leap of Elizabeth's heart at the sound of Mary's voice. Freud has made explicit what every mother instinctively knows: her child's character is already forming and reacting to the environment of her body and soul.

13

Once out of the womb, the child feels the intimacy of the father's protective arms, strong voice, and reassuring laugh. From its mother's breast-milk, her softer voice, and her cuddling, the child feels gentle faithfulness. The Arab children of the Holy Land reveal, in their confident friendliness, how intimately they have been touched by their parents, brothers, and sisters. Unlike animals, the human child is terribly and beautifully dependent for some years on its family, especially in our present technological civilization. Recall the newspaper picture of the policeman tenderly holding the tearful, frightened abandoned child as it clings to him; the child needs intimacy even from a uniformed stranger.

But intimacy not only creates us, it continually fosters us through various intimate processes. Learning a language enables the child to express its own inner life and to enter into the lives of others. As the child learns new words, feels the control which they give it over its own life and the lives of others, finds itself growing in knowledge, it becomes exuberant with this new intimacy. One has only to observe the child made isolate by its deafness and dumbness to know by contrast what intimacy does for a child. At the other end of the life-spectrum the elderly, growing gradually deafer and watching their world slip farther and farther away, value all the more the opportunities for intimate communication by word and touch.

In the next stage, the child's basic education becomes more sophisticated as the child moves out of its home and neighborhood-block into the classroom. The child learns quickly the limits of family intimacy in the first playground fight. In contrast with this bigger world, the child comes to treasure more the smaller world of family living, of being cared for by older brothers and sisters, of playing with younger brothers and sisters, of imitating his father and mother in telling a witty story, in giving gifts generously, and in disciplining justly the wayward. The child may at times envy the one-child family when he or she has been chastened for bad behavior; but later the child estimates this differently after recognizing the loneliness and, perhaps, self-centeredness of the "only child."

Then, through the process of making acquaintances and friends outside the family circle, the child turns into the adolescent. The shared entertainment of movies, television, museums, zoos, and sports gradually acclimates the adolescent to companionship not dictated by family living. The boys' gang and the girls' clique teach the rudiments of friend-making and underline the sad instances of the lonely and the companionless who wander idly through life, empty, bored, and vulnerable to drugs, alcohol and abuse. For these latter, the process of making friends and of learning intimacy outside the family has turned into a tragic denial of any intimacy.

In later adulthood, one's faithful friend or two, along with the family, commiserate one's sorrows or defeats and celebrate one's joys and successes. In this way, the intimacy of friendship gradually deepens its roots in the warm, fertile soil of mutual lasting affection and love. Thus the growth of intimacy is recognized to be face-to-face living with the friend in daily contact. As a result, gradually, almost imperceptibly like osmosis, the fruits of friendship ripen into quiet enjoyment of each other's presence, sure support of one another, penetrating understanding of each other's strengths and weaknesses, deep mutual affection, and such trust that each can challenge the other without fear of friendship-loss.[2]

But not only have we been created by intimacy and developed into adulthood through intimacy-processes, we also have been destined for intimacy. In astonishing ways beyond our soaring expectations, intimacy is the final goal of our total being. For God wishes to be intimate with us in at least five major ways. First of all, there is an unexpected satisfaction in praying with God; we find ourselves at home there no matter where we may be. Prayer centers us so that our life takes on meaning, direction, and purpose. Second, such prayer life finds it roots in the sacraments since they are seven moments when God enters one's life with particular intimacy: birth, adolescence, lethal sin, marriage, ordination to priesthood, sickness-death, and Eucharistic living.[3] These events may be peak-or valley-experiences; in either instance God is with us, Emmanuel.

There is yet a third major way in which God becomes deeply present to us: namely when he is forming his family through our service and sacrifice. "As often as you did it for one of my least brothers, you did it for me," is meant to let us know that he is compenetrating the *anawim* whom we attempt to serve; we touch him in them. In fact, they also touch him in us. Fourth, we may fall in love with Christ through meditative contemplation of the Gospel scenes. This means that awareness of the risen Christ (the living Gospel) within us—his insights, values, hopes, charming ways—will so deeply possess us that our decisions will inevitably form the intimate family of God, the Church or people of Christ.[4]

This intimacy would seem to be the finest of all if it were not revealed to us by Christ that there is a fifth way he wishes to be intimate with us. After death we enter into the fullest family life of the Trinity and form a complete family with all other people saved by the death and resurrection of Christ. Consequently, not only will this intimacy with God never end, but it will continue to grow ever deeper forever. No wonder that our hunger for intimacy is unrelenting and our fear of it so often overwhelming. We are made for divine intimacy. Who would not be restless with anything less than this and who would not, at the same time, be fearful of it? We well understand Augustine's remark to Christ: "Our hearts are restless until they rest in you."

2. Jesus Became Intimate with the Father through Prayer

Lest we become discouraged about getting to know God intimately through the daily prayer of intimacy, Jesus Christ showed us how it was to be done: face-to-face, alone, daily, and gradually. Luke the evangelist tells us: "Great crowds gathered to hear him and to be cured of their maladies. He often retired to deserted places and prayed" (5:15–16). Jesus retired in this manner at his baptism (Lk 3:21), in the desert temptations (Lk 4:1), just before selecting the twelve apostles

(Lk 5:15–16), after confronting the Pharisees (Lk 6:12), and when secluded before Peter's confession of faith (Lk 9:18). At the major turns in his apostolic life, Jesus met his God face-to-face where there was no room for dodging responsibilities, no chance to escape intense personal commitment, no opportunity to dissemble one's true feelings. This prayer of Jesus was characterized by aloneness and by daily gradual growth.

This is the prayer of day-to-day intimacy which happens not just on holidays, nor merely amid crises, nor simply when one feels moved to it. It is like the day-to-day intimacy of family life around the breakfast table, the shared car or bathroom, the family television set, the evening dinner, the family squabbles and the persistent financial worries. Such intimacy demands strict honesty. The praying person must be willing to speak out his or her anger at God directly, to admit faults, to own sins, and to be alertly grateful for talents, friends and opportunities to serve others.

In face-to-face daily prayer such as this, one must be content to be alone. But like Moses on Mount Sinai and like Elijah and Jeremiah, we are frightened at being alone with God; he is fearsome to us. To find all God's attention focused on oneself alone is to feel like Voltaire on an Alpine peak watching the sun rise in splendor. We, too, go down on our knees—if we are not simply casual. Thus it is easier at times to hide in spontaneous group prayer or in liturgy or in family prayer or in prayer of the apostolic moment. The trouble is that all these forms of prayer get their vitality from the day-to-day, lonely prayer of intimacy.

Because of our fear of being alone with God, we can attempt to escape the daily call of this prayer of intimacy even though it is clear to us that intimacy comes only from the saturating experience of hours and hours of prayer with God. The prayer of day-to-day intimacy is not a "quick fix" where we pass the Lord quickly with a fleeting smile, a casual wave of the hand, the abbreviated greeting: "Hi, Lord," and the swift return to the task at hand. The Lord has told us: "No one knows the Father except the Son and those to whom the

Son reveals the Father" (Mt 11:27; Lk 10:22). Now what son
can tell you about his father in merely occasional five-minute
snippets—especially if his father happens to be more than
finite? The way each of us has been constituted by, through,
and for intimacy makes it clear that intimacy must be daily,
face-to-face, alone, saturated with experiences of the dear
one.

   If we happen to doubt that intimacy grows slowly, we
should take a long look at the slow history of our friendships.
Rarely, if ever, are they instant like our coffee, tea, and
orange juice. Rather they are slow and gradual. The song from
the play *Godspell* puts this so well: "Day by day, day by day,
O dear Lord, three things I pray: to see thee more clearly,
love thee more dearly, follow thee more nearly, day by day."
For at the heart of intimacy is trust and how slowly trust is
given to another and how carefully it is distilled out of a
thousand incidents. For intimacy involves the increasing
willingness to suffer for the friend, to be patient with the
friend's weaknesses, to help with the friend's burdens, and to
be changed by the friend's needs. Intimacy seems hardly the
place to which we madly flee; it is more the place from which
we swiftly escape.

   The prayer of day-to-day intimacy, then, is at least as
demanding as friendship but also as rewarding. In fact it is the
most rewarding of all types of prayer since it is their taproot.
The problem, however, is that, as in friendship, the reward
takes a long time to show itself in our experience; but the
demands are there right from the beginning. Where do we get
the courage and the wisdom, then, to continue day-to-day
prayer through the desert years? For like any good marriage
or friendship, there are long periods of emotional dryness, of
boring ordinariness, of misunderstanding, and of unexpected
flare-ups. How do we keep patience long enough for the
rewarding intimacy with God to occur?

3. Sources of Strength for Following Christ to the Father

   There are four sources of strength and wisdom for making
the long journey into intimacy with the Father: the sacrament

of baptism, the mysteries of Christ's Gospel, the daily prayer of intimacy, and honest questioning of God. Baptism does for each of us what nothing else can do. We thereby begin the day-to-day family life of the Trinity, Father, Son and Spirit. Once one recognizes that all the millions of years of the evolving universe and all human history are simply the gradual exteriorization of the Trinity's inner life, then one also sees that at any one moment the infinite and eternal richness of this inner life is being spelled out in the slow motion of evolution and history. At this point one glimpses the awesome richness of that Trinitarian life into which the sacrament of baptism lifts us.

As if this were not enough, baptism also renders us truly brothers and sisters of Christ. This is not merely a pretty metaphor coined by overly zealous preachers. It is a solid fact that we Christians have a family life with Christ (now the spouse of the baptized person) and with our fellow Christians (now our brothers and sisters through Christ). This reassures us that Christ uniquely cares for each of us, that we are precious in his eyes, that he would be quite willing to die for us again, should this be necessary. For his love is not poured out like a stream of water from a firehouse indiscriminately flooding us. Instead his love is like a gentle spring rain seeking out each seed and tendril for delicate gifting.[5]

In other words, we simultaneously enjoy individual and familial life in the Trinity and in the people of God, Christ's Church; we are not treated like "the masses." Both levels of this family life are day-to-day, gradually growing, confrontive (face-to-face), and, finally, demanding individual response from each of us. For this family life, by some paradox, will require from time to time that its individual member stand alone with Christ as Peter failed to do in the courtyard of Caiaphas and as he succeeded in doing when confronting the Sanhedrin after Pentecost (Acts 4:19; 5:29) and when enduring his crucifixion in Rome. The prayer of day-to-day intimacy is, indeed, lonely at times.

In addition to baptism, a second source of strength for this prayer is the mysteries of Christ's Gospel-life as they occur not merely in the pages of the Gospel book, but more

importantly in one's prayer experience. If St. Paul is right that
the Gospel is actually the presence of the risen Christ within
each Christian (Rom 1:4 16; 1 Cor 15:1–2), then to scan the
pages of the Gospel is really to implicitly ask Christ to relive
his Gospel memories within one's praying. Indeed, these
memories grow more vibrant over the years as their fuller
meaning and impact become better appreciated by Christ and
by the person praying them with Christ. Like a good brother,
Christ relives these memories not just in his own memory and
actions but also in those of his praying brother or sister. Thus
the latter and Christ share their deepest values and hopes
enshrined in these memories, much as an engaged couple
would do. For this reason, Christ's earliest memories, the
Gospel, are more alive now than in the first century because
they are growing richer in the human memory of Christ. They
are more fully developed because they are being shared with
more and more Christians as the latter live out these vibrant
Gospel memories with Christ in their own century and
historical milieu.[6]

Such sharing of life with Christ enlivens the day-to-day
prayer of intimacy which then becomes the third source of
greater intimacy with the Father. For his beloved Son, in
becoming more and more real in the praying person's
experience, more and more powerfully reveals his Father.
Though this prayer of intimacy is often dramatized in the
back-pew, head-in-hands posture of seemingly desperate
petition, it is also, often enough, a prayer of quiet serenity, of
undramatic ordinariness, of humdrum dryness. Yet it
nonetheless exercises a strange attraction on us. For, whatever
its posture and profile, this prayer lends a growing stability to
one's life. In the praying person there is a sense of being at
home, of having the center of the universe within oneself, of
knowing something of the world's direction, of having one's
fears about job-family-country-neighborhood reduced. One
experiences in a vague yet powerful way that Christ was not
speaking jocularly when he said: "If anyone loves me and the
Father, we will come to him and make our home with him"
(Jn 14:23).

Because of this "at homeness" with God, one can ask those shockingly honest questions common among friends. This is the fourth source of strength for doing the day-to-day prayer of intimacy with God. It is not easy at first to ask questions of the Lord such as these: "Lord, why do you love me?" (He might just tell me.) "If you do love me, why have you let this happen to me?" (His silence can be deafening, they say.) "Where were you yesterday when . . . ?" (He might ask a question himself: "And what were you thinking about when you . . . ?") The Lord likes us to ask shocking questions: "Who is my mother, my brother, my sister? The one who keeps my commandments, my word" (Lk 8:19–21). Such questions and answers are the mark of great confidence in a human friendship. Why not also in a divine friendship? Do not these questions so assume the depth of the mutual love that their very asking increases that love? For this reason, we can afford to get very angry with a close friend because our trust in the strength of the friendship is so high. Is one's trust in God's friendship to be less high?[7]

If we are created by, through, and for intimacy so that it constitutes our very being, if human intimacy is meant to be crowned by divine intimacy, if baptism, Gospel mystery, daily prayerful facing of Christ, and confidence to ask shocking questions assure one of greater intimacy with the Father, then why do we at times seemingly dread being alone, face-to-face with the Lord for fifteen minutes? There does seem to be an inhibiting fear of aloneness. Christ himself knew what this fear was. If his three temptations were truly temptations and not merely artificial charades, he felt the desert loneliness of finding out the Father's will for himself. Again, the night before he chose his apostles (Lk 5:15–16), his prayer with the Father must have seemed long and tortuous. In a third instance, when Christ stood alone before the people of Nazareth (Lk 4:14–30) to be rejected and almost killed by them, prayer with the Father must have appeared dangerous. Certainly, as he prayed alone in Gethsemane with the apostles asleep, he must have felt a dereliction comparable only to that of his next day's prayer on the cross: "My God, my God, why have you forsaken me (left me an orphan)?" (Mk 15:34).

Christ's day-to-day life of prayer with the Father seems to say to us that loneliness is necessary for growth in intimacy with himself and the Father. Is Christ saying to us: "If you cannot stand yourself for long, how can you stand anyone else for long?" Or is he rather saying: "I am with you all days to the end of the world. Take heart, my heart"?[8]

Stage Three
Prayer of Forgiveness:
The Impossible Pain of Intimacy[1]

Because only those dear to us can hurt us deeply and unforgettably, the act of forgiving a close friend can be an excruciating intimacy. The shattered mind of the forgiver must be pieced together again and the crushed heart must learn to expand again. The forgiver, in other words, has to rebuild the world of understanding splintered at its center by the betrayer. The forgiver has also to let the heart be healed so that it can expand to include the forgiven person once again. What a price to pay! Yet Christ claims in the Our Father that this forgiveness is essential if one wishes to come into contact with the Father, if one wishes to pray (Mt 6:8–14; cf. also Mt 5:23–26: "If you bring your gift to the altar and there recall that your brother has anything against you . . . go first to be reconciled").

Then, too, Christ's portrait of the forgiving Christian mesmerizes us: "Love your enemies . . . pray for those who maltreat you . . . turn the other cheek" (Lk 6:27–29). We shake our heads and try to explain away this impossibly demanding challenge to our human feelings. For this reason people rightly wonder about Pope John Paul II's forgiveness of his assassin, Ali Agca.[2] How real can this be? What does it mean to forgive? How could prayer ever enable a person to offer such forgiveness? Once I, the so-called forgiver, dare to review the rogues' gallery of those whom I have failed to forgive or did forgive reluctantly, I have good reason to shudder at the hidden mines which lurk in the depths of forgiveness and which are set, it would seem, to explode the forgiving person into shreds.

23

1. A Realistic Appraisal of What Forgiveness Is

If one's evaluation of forgiveness dishonestly underestimates the cost, then one risks making a superficial act of forgiveness, an act easily made and just as easily forgotten. Thus it must be clear from the outset that to forgive is not to forget. Rather it is to remember a hurt unforgettable because so deep and lasting. Simply to forget a hurt is simply to suppress its remembrance (or never to have been hurt in the first place). But suppression, far from freeing one of the hurt, merely drives the remembrance of the hurt deep into one's unconscious where it can secretly dominate one's reactions toward "the enemy" and even toward other unforgiven enemies. For example, I can play the passive-aggressive role against the enemy by not answering her letters, by cooperating very slowly and half-heartedly in a common project with her, by unobtrusively denigrating her character with a lifted eyebrow when someone attempts to praise her. I avenge myself with mean but subtle domination; I punish her well. This attitude can then transfer its venom to her innocent family and friends—without my being aware of it. Therefore to forgive is not to forget, nor to suppress, if the hurt is deep enough to be always remembered.

But, then, what is forgiveness taken positively? There would appear to be four stages in a full act of forgiveness. The first is not to wish evil on the one who has hurt me, not to take revenge in any way. This may not seem to be much, but without this step, forgiveness never begins. The second stage is to reaffirm the worth of the offender with an act of trust in him or her. This act of trust is based not only on the offender's goodness but on the assurance that God's assistance will be given to both the forgiver and the offender. This trust, however, is not blind; it must take into account the offender's ignorance, compulsions, lack of sensitivity, and previous offenses. Otherwise, one foolishly neglects the natural defense-mechanisms in oneself, and this is to risk all future acts of forgiveness. For one becomes disheartened by past unrealistic acts of forgiveness which ended in depressing frustrations. Thus Christ, in asking us to be as simple as doves, at the same time requires us to be as prudent as serpents.

The third stage of forgiveness puts an ache in every bone: it is to restore the offender to one's circle of acquaintances or friends. Sometimes this requires all the delicate diplomacy of a Luxemburg foreign minister talking simultaneously to Hitler and Stalin. False warmth, condescension, sarcasm, or unintentional slight can each and all make the hurt worse. So, a fourth stage of forgiveness is often necessary: to recall Christ's suggestion that the forgiver must be ready to repeat his or her act of forgiveness seventy times seven times if the offender asks forgiveness each time (Mt 18:21–22). The repentant son or daughter who has torn the family apart with cocaine use must be most delicately enfolded into the family. But amid repeated forgiveness, there must be clear, agreed limits of tolerance lest the offender lose dignity and family ties be shredded.

Consequently, within the forgiving person, there can occur a magnificent growth of compassion for the offender— at no small cost. For forgiveness without compassion becomes a routine act, sometimes more damaging than healing. The offender must know that the forgiving person understands the offender's weakness and enters into it in the act of forgiving. Otherwise, the offender may feel patronized and soon turn into the naughty little boy or girl whose mean behavior is either ignored as inconsequential or accepted like the act of other little animals. Thus the act of forgiveness must be free of revenge, affirming of the offender's worth, restorative of his or her place in the acquaintance circle, and thoroughly patient without condescension. Such an act is as painful as it is magnificent.

Because all this costs so much, the forgiving person must be given time, much time, to forgive. Though occasionally a friendship disrupted by deep hurt may be deepened by the forgiveness, often the reunion, no matter how beautiful, contains lessened trust. For a natural psychological protection-mechanism allows trust to be restored only gradually and never in the same way as previous to the deep hurt. For example, the priest knocks on the front door of the apartment and Barbara invites him in. The priest glances around the living room at the small piano with the family portraits on it—the happier days—and says: "Barbara, let me speak quickly and directly. Bill wants to return to you and the family." Barbara's eyes fill up, her mouth tightens: "Father, I knew the day before yesterday why you were asking to see me and I've been thinking of this possibility the past forty-eight hours. I will accept Bill back, if only for the children's sake. But things will never be the same. How could they?" Yet her eyes implore the priest: "Tell me that I'm wrong." The wise priest will not tell her that she is wrong; he will only suggest that forgiving takes time and eventually does bring some healing—with God working harder than both the forgiver and the offender to heal their shattered love.

Sometimes, during the long forgiving process, the betrayal-event may come to be more fully understood in all its horror and so the hurt is increased during the forgiving time. Because the hurt is growing, the forgiving is never quite over; there is always a need for increasing acceptance. The young daughter in the Alanon group becomes more and more aware of the damage done the family by her alcoholic father. Forgiveness must be given over and over again as her therapy continues through the months. A priest, ordained in the late 1950's, watched one-third of his ordination class leave the priesthood to marry; he felt a mounting anger. Depression grew as he realized that, because of these defections, parishes would be understaffed, people needing counsel would not receive it, the sick in the hospitals would receive fewer visits, youth would not find ready encouragement amid their problems. Besides, he himself felt rejected by these friends. Could he forgive? And if he did forgive once, would he have to keep forgiving again and again as he saw people unattended again and again because of the priest-shortage and as he felt the pain of his friends' supposed rejection more and more acutely over the years? Is this the meaning of the Lord's response to Peter: "Yes, forgive seventy times seven times"?

There is a third reason why forgiveness takes such a long time: it occurs in all three dimensions of the forgiving person's being. For example, the rape-victim is asked to forgive her assailant. Physically, her body has been violated and punished by a total stranger (or, worse, by someone whom she had trusted). She may even compulsively take long showers to rid herself of the feeling of being filthy. Psychologically, her emotions may become deranged toward the sexual act (as merely the thought of it raises terrible memories), toward her fiancé or husband (as she worries whether she is to be considered damaged goods), toward her friends (as she demands more, and gets less, attention during the ensuing weeks). Spiritually, if she has experienced the slightest pleasure in the act of rape, she will wonder about her integrity. If she wonders long enough, she becomes filled with a haunting false guilt: was there something seductive about her that led the rapist to consider her an easy mark?

All three interacting dimensions of her personality must be first healed before forgiveness can make much sense to the victim, as she struggles with thoughts of revenge, human respect, and spiritual bankruptcy. This all takes time. Each of us knows how long it takes because, along life's road, each of us has been metaphorically raped, e.g., by a mean situation easily remediable but never remedied by those responsible for it, by the business associate who took financial advantage of us, by the manipulative superior officer who overworked us to accelerate his career–climb, by the parent who wanted to live his or her dreams in our sport success or in our college popularity as did Willy Loman in *Death of a Salesman*.

Forgiveness, then, is a mysterious action. It requires remembrance rather than forgetting, a trusting reintroduction of the offender into one's circle rather than a freezing out, an acceptance of healing in all dimensions of the forgiver's personality rather than a cultivating of wounds, and a long-time supporting of the will to forgive rather than short patience. Christian forgiveness is, then, terribly demanding. How is this seemingly impossible act made possible?

2. Sources of Strength for Reconciling Forgiveness

If sacrament and Scripture are not allowed to strengthen the forgiver, then full forgiveness of deep hurt becomes a rare event. For these are the principal sources of generous forgiveness and, through them, comes the prayer of forgiveness (which is of immediate importance for strengthening the forgiving act). For both sources are to be taken as the presence of the risen Christ working within us. To understand this, let us look at the forgiveness of serious sin in the sacrament of reconciliation. The strengthening presence of Christ within the sinner as he or she approaches the sacrament shows in the sense of sorrow for sin, in the reconciliation with the person offended by one's sin, and hence in restored union with the Christian community. All this enables the sinner to again become intimate with Christ as Brother and with Yahweh as Father. Here the intimacy takes the form of an assurance: "Yes, I am loved by the Son and the Father. In fact, because of their faithfulness, I never lost that love; I simply cut it off deliberately with my sins while they continued to love me." A second and remarkable assurance is included in the reconciliation: "Yes, I can live faithfully with this regained intimacy of Christ and the Father; I am not doomed inescapably to another serious betrayal of their trust in me."

But it is not enough for the sinner to know reconciliation; he or she must feel it, must experience reconciliation with that community against which the serious betrayal has been committed. The sinner, in other words, must know in his or her bones that he or she is back home again, safe within the family of fellow sinners. In this way, the forgiveness of each other makes the sacrament of reconciliation felt. This can occur when the thrice divorced woman's return to the Church is symbolized by her friends' joy at her conversion, by their new interest in her health and financial security, and by their invitations into social circles. This sacramental rejoining of the community happens, too, when the convict is welcomed back into the family, finds himself relaxing again with the

neighbors, and is offered a job by one of the parishioners.
Now the efficacious presence of Christ in the community is
felt working both in the sinner and in the forgiving
community.

This is not, however, an automatic process. I, the sinner,
come to better appreciate the gift in the sacrament, when I
am called upon to show the same mercy to others as I have
received from the Lord and from the community against
whom I sinned. I am now called to pass this mercy on to
others, that is, to forgive as I was forgiven earlier. This can be
a harsh experience for me because I find myself unable to
match the generous trust of those who have forgiven me
previously. Here any lofty snobbery on my part is brought
down to earth, grounded in the reality of my need to grow
much in the intimate experience of forgiving others. I must
learn to forgive even myself for being so much less than I had
previously supposed.

Thus if I am the priest who attempts marriage with a
young parishioner, my healing occurs when I swallow my
pride and seek forgiveness of the scandalized parishioners and
of the desolate family of the young woman. But the healing is
not completed until I make amends to the young woman, until
I am received back into the circle of my priest friends, until I
am once again accepted by the parish members whom I
depressed with my disloyalty, and until my bishop arranges
for me to return to priestly work. Here, the Lord is seen as
the one who underlies and supports all acts of forgiveness and
sorrow in the community.

But this reconciliation from serious sin is seen as only the
beginning of one's growth. For it is in the forgiveness of less
serious sin that the challenge to growing intimacy with Christ
and with the community is heard more clearly. This growth,
gradual-tortuous-demanding, occurs first of all in the offended
person who keeps on forgiving the offending sinner even
though the hurt may have deepened, even though the healing
is so complex in all its dimensions, even though the offender
may never learn to appreciate fully the cost of the
forgiveness. Secondly, the slow expansion of mind and heart

also happens in the sinner when I, the sinner, discover what forgiveness demands of me, not merely from my own failings to forgive but more importantly from Christ's continuing forgiveness of me day-by-day, face-to-face, in the midst of my backsliding, unending excuses, recurrent weaknesses. The sacrament of reconciliation never stops operating in the life of both forgiver and offender. For Christ's faithful presence adapts to all their unique "ups and downs" day-to-day. The sacrament is never quite finished for them so long as they ask for help. After all, if Christ has asked of us that we forgive seventy times seven times, he himself could hardly do less, given his great heart and deep understanding.

There is a second major source of strength for the sinner who is trying to reach oneness with Christ and his community: the scriptural word. Here Christ shows his tender toughness not only on the printed page of the New Testament, but more particularly in the sinner's spiritual experience where the risen Christ makes himself and his Gospel message heard and felt.[3] It is not enough to read the mercy parables in the fifteenth chapter of Luke's Gospel. The reader must experience the merciful reality of the lost sheep recovered, of the widow's coin regained, of the prodigal son forgiven and celebrated for his return. Only the risen Christ inhabiting the very being of the sinner can flood his mind with the fact of God's mercy and open his heart to embrace Christ himself.

At that cosmic moment the sinner knows and feels forgiven by God so that he or she can accept the forgiveness of the community and then can give this same mercy to others. Then Christ's remark to the Pharisee host in defense of Mary Magdalene rings the mind and heart of the sinner: "Her many sins are forgiven because of her great love" (Lk 7:47). For Christ, the act of continuing forgiveness is a source of ever new and deeper intimacy between him and the sinner, no matter how many the sins, so long as the sinner wants to reform. For unlike us (recall the disheartened Barbara and the righteous priest), God is always faithful, always trustworthy, always waiting for intimate exchange, always ready to forgive far beyond seventy times seven times.

If you doubt this, consider the volcanic Christ pouring the lava of his burning words upon the Pharisees in the six great woes (Mt 23:13–36) and then lamenting in the next event (Mt 23:37) as he overlooks his city: "Jerusalem, Jerusalem, murderess of prophets and stoner of those who were sent to you. How often have I yearned to gather your children, as a mother bird gathers her young under wings, but you refused me." Somehow under his anger there is always the compassion of his mercy; under his so-called declaration of war on the Pharisees, a call to the intimacy which only a mother can give to the children of her sorrow.

Indeed, God is the master of final irony. Through my sins, once forgiven, I can save others from their sins as Psalm 51 hints. Just as the reformed alcoholic is the best savior of the struggling drunkard, so the life of a great sinner like Charles de Foucauld can offer the surest hope to sinners walking in the desert of despair. The reformed alcoholic and Foucauld make salvation through Christ more believable. For this reason, Paul of Tarsus was convinced that Christ had forgiven Paul's persecution of the Church and other grand sins so that no sinner would ever have reason to doubt the depth of Christ's willingness to forgive (1 Tim 1:15–16).

Because Christ's presence in the sacrament guarantees reconciliation of sinner with God and community, because Christ's risen presence within the reader of Scripture enables the latter to understand and feel the reality of the forgiving Word, therefore full forgiveness becomes possible for both the forgiver and the offender no matter how great the sin. The tender toughness of Christ is alive in sacrament and word to heal the offender and the forgiver. But what brings this intimacy immediately into the life of forgiver and offender is the prayer of forgiveness. For the latter demands much intimacy of its very nature.

3. Prayer of Forgiveness Offers Intimacy

To understand and live the prayer of forgiveness, one must see how it works before, during and after the "enemy"

Dark Intimacy

is forgiven. Before I can forgive the offender, I must pray to
still the hostile reactions from the hurt endured. I find myself
conducting imaginary dialogues with the offender in which
the latter is made to feel my anger and vengeance. In these
internal hostile exchanges, even God is not spared; my anger
lashes out at him if the hurt is deep. At times I may have to
acknowledge that I cannot now forgive the enemy even if God
were to intervene. Indeed, the drive to take revenge is
pulsing strongly. I need time to mull the events and to gather
together the fragments of my life and person. The healing
process demands some rest for both forgiver and offender.

At this point I need to ask God to forgive me my desire to
avenge the wrong; I have to accept for the moment my stark
inability to even begin to forgive the offender. Instead, I must
forgive myself for this desire for vengeance and for the violent
anger against God who has not done things as I wanted them
done. To start to forgive myself here is to start to forgive God
and the offender.[4] For the hardest person to forgive is usually
oneself especially since one does not trust oneself to stay
worthy of forgiveness for a very long time.[5]

If through prayer I am beginning to move toward
forgiveness, then my prayer of forgiveness starts to become a
request of God that I do not weaken in my resolve to forgive
the offender. Perhaps I have finally seen that to refuse
forgiveness is to be imprisoned in my own bitterness, that
vengeance locks me into the always escalating "tit for tat,"
that this becomes the nightmare of discovering more and
more enemies with whom to lock in combat. This is the
demonic world from which Christ came to liberate me by his
own bloody murder at the hands of forgiven sinners: "Father,
forgive them; they do not know what they are doing" (Lk
23:34).[6]

If such demanding prayer precedes the act of forgiveness,
then it will continue during the act where, in forgiving, I can
now become aware that God is within me and stilling my
vengeance with remembrance of his own death to vengeance.
At this point I might notice that God is also present within the
offender so that our reconciliation is sealed with Christ's

blood. Such a presence makes the embarrassment and awkwardness of reconciliation bearable. It further enables me, the forgiver, to recall some of the good qualities of the offender to which I had been blinded by sheer pain.

If my prayer of forgiveness perdures through the act of forgiveness, then very likely it will continue in me so that I can be patient with the offender's acceptance of forgiveness (casual? overly grateful? too embarrassed?). If this be true, then I can hold back any reawakened feelings of vengeance. This same patience is needed to await the growth of grace in both the offender and the forgiver so that the necessarily slow healing can occur. Now after the forgiving act, the problem is to let one's actions communicate benevolence and hope to the offender—especially when the old spirit of vengeance resurfaces. Prayer of forgiveness must remain vigilant lest the praying person slip back into vengefulness, into ugly meanness of thought and action, into the dark bitterness of disdain for the offender.

4. The Unforgivable Person

But such prayer is challenged most by the shocking situation where the offender seems totally unaware of having hurt me. How do I forgive the brother who has systematically belittled me over many years but who is dumbfounded when I finally protest with scalding words? In defense, he accuses me of always disliking him for no good reason; then he stalks out of my life. Or how forgive the father, long dead, who during life pursued financial power twenty-four hours per day and left the family virtually fatherless? How can Christian forgiveness even get started if reciprocal sorrow and forgiveness are impossible?

These two instances make it clear that, when my natural, retaliatory defense is already working, I need God's grace even to start the process of forgiving. Do I even want "to want to forgive"? Is not Christian forgiveness impossible in this instance? Yet why cannot Christ do reciprocal healing simply between himself and me? Here Christ would do all the

healing since the offender's sorrow for my hurt, a normal
source of healing, would be absent. Christ should be expert at
this type of solitary healing because he knew in his public life
and passion how it felt to receive not the slightest apology for
attacks on his person.

The uncomprehending offender, therefore, dramatizes for
us that Christ is always the principal healer and that he
endures some pain in forgiving our partially unknowing
offenses against others and himself. May not this situation also
sensitize us to our own foibles and sins which only add to the
bitterness of our hurt and which may even blind us to the hurt
we have caused others? Perhaps within the unrecognized and,
therefore, seemingly unforgivable hurt lies the mystery of
forgiveness. Is it possible that the act of Christian forgiveness
is simply an invitation to the offender to recognize his or her
injury of the forgiver, to take stock of its destructiveness, to
let sorrow rise at the hurt done to the forgiver, to accept full
responsibility, and to humbly ask forgiveness? This would be
an invitation without demands, without hidden "shoulds"
attached for trussing up the offender. This would be an
invitation for the offender to grow in compassion, to re-enter
the life of the one offended, to form community (Church), and
to suffer the gritty love which alone brings final joy and
intimacy.[7]

If forgiving, then, is an invitation to the offender to grow
into fuller manhood or womanhood, its very allowance of
freedom to the offender to express or not to express sorrow
shows how the act of forgiving can occur even when the
offender is only superficially aware of guilt or totally unaware
of having hurt the forgiver. The invitation itself is a new
nobility in the forgiver no matter what happens in the
offender. Even more, it is a deeper union with the crucified
and risen Christ—a union which patiently waits for the
offender to reach awareness. This waiting, of course, requires
a strong act of faith in the Lord's graceful presence and in the
offender's latent goodness.[8]

The alternative to offering Christian forgiveness is to hang
onto one's hurts and to let them embitter the heart so that

eventually one rigidly refuses to allow for people's diverse levels of sensitivity, depths of ignorance, and ways of appreciating the need to seek forgiveness. One thus becomes untouchably self-righteous. This posture seems to forget the fact that the Lord Jesus, being fully human, did not find it easy to forgive—as though, being divine, he could brush off hurts like road-dust. For actually his sensitivity was enhanced by the fact that he was divine as well as human in his knowledge, feelings, hopes and willingness to trust. As a matter of fact, his hurts are more unforgettable than ours because the Gospel events of his suffered indignities are actually immortal memories contained in his risen personality. This means that he is still forgiving, in the 1980's and 1990's, these events of two thousand years ago. His prayer of forgiveness, then, perdures and grows ever wider and deeper as the centuries pass. Such, too, may well be our own prayer of forgiveness as we move to ever deeper stages of intimacy.[9]

5. Conclusion

This terribly difficult prayer of forgiveness is worth all the pain it costs. For not rarely it changes the forgiver much more than the one forgiven. Slowly it dawns on the forgiver that he or she can hardly appreciate what it means to be forgiven by Christ until having suffered the pain of forgiving someone dear. It becomes clear, too, in the heart of the forgiver how searing is the intimacy of forgiveness for God and for the offender and how love for them is the only reason for such forgiveness. Merely strategic or manipulative forgiveness is seen as the basest betrayal of trust.

Now the Our Father cannot be said without a twinge of pain and a sense of intimacy between the forgiver, the offender, and God the Father. Now the sacrament of reconciliation is appreciated for its terrible demands and its magnificent promises; it does form a community of love and each member must suffer this love intensely through communion in each other's pains and sorrows. Now the prayer of forgiveness is found to be a prayer of remembrance, either rueful or peaceful, either haunting in guilt or reassuring in forgiveness, either a mere psychological trick or a sacrament bearing the forgiving Christ within it. These fearsome options are open to one's own free choice as one prays before, during, and after the act of forgiveness.

Stage Four
Prayer of Admitted Sinfulness: Healing Ruptured Intimacy[1]

Despite all the newspaper headlines garishly describing a thousand daily sins, the meaning of sin has lately been obscured and the fact of human sinfulness has consequently been underestimated.[2] As a result human consciousness has become confused and, at times, even panicky. Indeed, if sin happens to be rupture of intimacy between persons, then to underestimate it is to risk serious personal damage the more intimate people are with each other. For intimacy would seem to be the state of living deeply in the life of the beloved by sharing joys, pleasures, pains, sorrows, ambitions, and hopes. If sin is the rupture of such intimacy, then the loss it causes to any human community is grievous and a healing process such as prayer of admitted sinfulness must be discovered.

But how can one become aware of such sin unless previously one knows what intimacy is and unless God has already forgiven our sins so that we know what reconciliation is? Could it be that the prayer of admitted sinfulness contains some revelation of what sin and reconciliation are, some sense of the intimacy which is violated by sin, and some power with which to heal this rupture? If so, it would pay us to reflect on this seemingly paradoxical prayer of admitted sinfulness. We do this by observing, first of all, how sin ruptures intimacy, secondly how revelation in word and sacrament can heal such ruptures, and finally how the sense of one's sinfulness (distinguished from the state of prayerlessness, but allied with the sacraments) can lead into the healing prayer of admitted sinfulness.

1. How Is Sin the Rupture of Intimacy?

If intimacy were found to be a creative union between persons, then its rupture would have dire consequences. To catalogue these consequences would be a negative way of appreciating the positive qualities of intimacy. How else do we deal with mysteries like intimacy and sin unless by this indirect approach? But the rupture of intimacy begins at levels below the personal and so we must first consider the fission of human beings from the physical, the vegetal, and the animal. For example, sin occurs at the physical level when a person treats things without respect, e.g., the wasting of food and water, the polluting of the atmosphere, the burning of timber tracts through negligence, the squandering of coal and oil resources, the destroying of buildings by arson, and the "garbaging" of parks, lakes, and rivers. For all these actions make it less and less possible for oneself and others to live in, with, and by these natural resources. Here one witnesses a divorce from creation. And how does one so disrespect creation without treating its Creator to the same scorn? These actions are called sins, therefore, not because we are writing dismal poetry but because they are actual ruptures from all that is beautiful and good and from the God who has generously poured his wisdom and love into these beauties and goods.

At another level, the vegetal, a second set of ruptures occurs when people treat living things as non-living. This, too, is a basic disrespect, a crude devaluing of life. To destroy crops for price supporting amid third world famines, to destroy flowerbeds out of pique or envy or sheer wantonness, to mutilate trees for vanity's sake or for show of power, to plant yet not to enrich the planting with water, are all actions indicating little appreciation for the struggle to live, little thought for the future beauty now blighted. As humans prostitute plant life to merely their own convenience and strange pleasure, they rupture their symbiotic union with plant life. Such union is dramatized by the person who has the green thumb, the person whose respect for life draws plants out into their full beauty and fruitfulness. Again, how can one explicitly scorn plant life without implicitly scorning the Giver of all life who in Genesis took such delight in all the variety of plants?

What has been said of things and plants is even more true of animals. C.S. Lewis in his *Problem of Pain* has noted that, by training an animal, one humanizes it.[3] On the one hand, the family dog may get the family ulcers but, on the other hand, he may feel the family joys and eagerly work at pleasing the family with every trick taught. Meanwhile, through this empathy between dog and master, the latter is also becoming more human. For, in respecting this animal, the master learns empathy with all animal life, respect for other types of life, and a sense of the unique gift which is each being's existence (no other dog will ever deliver a newspaper the way Ruffles does). Beatrix Potter, with her humanizing of animals in her life and books, has taught us the beauty of empathy with animal life. By contrast, one recognizes that cruelty to animals is truly a devastating rupture of such empathy and a short step away from cruelty to humans.

It is at the human level, however, where sin is most clearly seen as rupture, here the rupture of intimacy. For this break makes it impossible for people to live with each other except by armed truce since to rupture intimacy is inevitably to treat people as less than human. For example, the class clown is used by the class members for cheap entertainment and he or she unfortunately accepts the degrading role as the only one offered. The ambitious executive can use his wife as a clever hostess-entertainer for his business parties. The ego-maniac retains his "hangers-on" for their flattering attendance on him until he grows tired of their antics and expels them. The selling of fake insurance to the unwary poor and the paying of slave-wages to immigrants lacking visas are further ways of degrading others, of rupturing human relations with them. Soldiering on the assembly-line job and pressuring management for overpayment in wages and in fringe benefits produce gaping fissures of injustice in human society and incite rupturing hostility between management and worker, between company and its buying public.

In all these instances, we sinners are busy making it more difficult for ourselves and for others to be human. Our sins are deliberately debasing others as we systematically rupture the intimate union between persons, the union of mutual respect, support, confidence, and future hope in each other. This lowering of trust estranges us from one another and thus keeps us from becoming more personal. In other words, it tends to animalize us since we deny each other the qualities which render us human. In denying gentleness we affirm violence, in denying respect we affirm degradation of others, in denying justice we affirm unfairness, in denying hope to others we affirm their despair, in denying them opportunity for growth we affirm their dwarfing or retardation. Thus sin as the rupture of intimacy is eventually lethal.

The naturalist, however, logically denies the existence of sin because, as with B.F. Skinner, the human being is simply the sum of environmental forces (nothing more) and, if there is any rupture of intimacy, it is caused by environmental pressures, not by human freedom. Besides, intimacy takes for granted personal commitment up to death, and this makes sense only if there is life after death and if we are not merely a sack of compulsions to be manipulated into the perfect citizen.

For the atheistic humanist like Sartre, the individual person is the measure of all reality, and the liberty of intimacy is only what the individual decrees it to be since no creative God exists to guide and protect his creation from ethical buccaneers. Sin is not possible since rupture of intimacy is not an evil; it is the right of the supreme individual who as sole arbiter of personal destiny is obligated to no one, yet as the human substitute for God is obligated to everyone and everything. Thus to deny the possibliity of sin is to turn the human into a living Sartrean contradiction.[4]

On the other hand, according to Christian understanding, the rupture of intimacy between persons is a free act between people who are indebted both to each other and to God in trust and in love and who are meant to protect each other from harm—even at the expense of self. "There is no greater love than this: to lay down one's life for one's friends" (Jn 15:13). Thus only if the human being is free, responsible to

God, and committed naturally to noble service of others can sin exist.

To sum up, sin is present at four levels. It is a rupture with creation or with plant life or with animals or, especially, with fellow humans. It arises out of a basic disrespect, even scorn, for things, plants, animals and human beings.[5] Because it is the enemy of life, it tends to paralyze, if not destroy, the union among persons and with God. Ironically, to deny the reality of sin is implicitly to denigrate the noblest qualities of human beings: freedom, responsibility to God, commitment to sacrifice for others. Rightly does John, the writer of three New Testament Epistles, see denial of sin as blasphemous: "If we say we have never sinned, we make him [God] a liar" (1 Jn 1:10).

2. Revelation: God's Great Act of Intimacy

If sin is the rupture of intimacy and if God intends to repair this rupture not only between human beings but also between them, God, and the infrahuman world, then what will be his strategy? Is it possible that God's first strategic act to restore human unity and to reconcile humans with creation and himself would be divine revelation? After all, in revelation God does divulge his inner life, he does entrust this self-revelation to us, and he does gamble that we will accept this act of intimacy and divulge ourselves trustingly to him in a return gamble. Is this incipient union-through-revelation the first step in teaching us humans what sin is, what the rupture of intimacy is and how to repair this rupture through reconciliation? Thus revelation itself would be at once an act of repairing the rupture and a description of what the rupture of intimacy is between humans and between them, God, and world.

And, surprisingly, this is exactly what the Genesis narrative shows itself to be: both an act of reconciliation and a description of the original rupture of intimacy between two humans and between them, God and the world. Notice how Adam and Eve, having partaken of the forbidden fruit, no

longer walk with the Lord in the garden during the cool of
the afternoon to share insights, hopes, stories of the day,
laughs and affection. Why? Because Adam and Eve are
ashamed of their treacherous act whereby they had hoped to
achieve the knowledge and the power promised them by the
serpent. This knowledge and power was to have made them
equal to God, in total control of their own lives, and capable
of challenging God. By establishing their independence from
God, they could have turned his friendship into a safer, more
manipulative acquaintanceship.

They lost, however, more than intimacy with God. They
lost intimacy with each other. No longer are Adam and Eve at
ease in each other's company. In a sharpened awareness of
their sexual drive and of its potential violence, they
awkwardly fashion loincloths for themselves. Then, fearful of
each other's newly found ability to betray, they take
distrustful measure of each other. Confrontation with God
finds Eve subtly complaining of the serpent's wiliness (a gift
from God) and reveals Adam explaining: "The woman whom
you put here with me, she gave me fruit from the tree" (Gen
3:12–13). They are now manipulative both of God and of
each other as each wonders how to protect the self against the
other's possible violence. For neither is about to accept
responsibility for the sins and to admit sinfulness. As a result,
they soon discover that they cannot protect Abel from Cain.
Intimacy has been, indeed, ruptured between them and God
and between all the human participants in the original
tragedy.

The rupture widens; even the fertile fields no longer are
united with humans. No longer will the earth yield its fruits
easily and gladly. Rather it bristles with briars and yields fruit
only after much back-breaking tilling, sowing, weeding and
harvesting. Man and woman now work with sweat, blood,
tears, and only an occasional smile. Thus the Genesis narrative
makes it clear that sin is the rupture of intimacy with persons,
of empathy with animals, and of cooperation with plants. The
flood of Noah's time will complete the drama of man's rupture
with all creation.

Now how will God work to repair the rupture, to restore the union between humans, creation, and himself, so that once again life can be wholesome? First of all, Yahweh promises a rescuer: "I will put enmity between you [the serpent] and the woman, and between your offspring and hers; he will strike at your head, while you strike at his heel" (Gen 3:15). Next, Yahweh thoughtfully makes leather garments for Adam and Eve (Gen 3:21). Then, after the flood, the Lord reestablishes human rapport with animals and plants, encourages humans to fill the earth, and makes an everlasting covenant with Noah and his descendants (Gen 8:15—9:17). Later, he restores religious intimacy when he leads Abram out of Haran into Canaan in order to instruct him about a certain God who is no mere function of nature but who is a personal father for Abram and his people.

Much later Yahweh works to restore fuller union between God and humans by helping Moses draft a covenant of friendship between God and humankind, not a covenant of slavery so popular among the pagan nations. Thus the Lord selects a people, calls them his chosen ones, leads them through a forty year "engagement period" in the Sinai desert and finally makes this people his own. "You are my people; I am your God" is the marriage formula echoing down through Old Testament history.[6]

Then, amid the fearsome demands and threats of Yahweh, come the tender revelations of the prophets Isaiah and Jeremiah that God is a gentle father to his children (Is 43:1–7; Jer 3:19; 31:8–9, 20), a rock of security and a champion for them (Is 17:10; 26:4; 44:8; Jer 3:14; 14:9; 20:11), a husband to his bride, Israel (Is 50:1; 54:5–10; 62:4–5; Jer 2:2; 3:1–4, 3:20; 11:15; 51:5). Here Hosea describes the marriage of Yahweh and his people in family terms of intimacy (2:18–22). This goes beyond mere friendship since marriage demands a deeper intimacy, a more terrible dependence.

But all this revelation of God's inner life and of his entrance into the personal history of a people is not enough. Next the Father sends his Christ into the womb of Mary, into the daily life of Nazareth, into the rich history of the Jewish people so that the Christ becomes totally a Jew (not the universal man of Hegel, but the one fully immersed in the Jewish attitudes and customs of the first century). Christ is the covenant with God's people in pulsing flesh. This covenant is no mere parchment, no great stone, no secret understanding between humans; it is Jesus summing up all previous Jewish history in his central nervous system. He is the vibrant marriage between God and humans; he is the perfect imaging of the Father. Thus this intimacy which is Jesus, the God-man incarnate, sums up and goes beyond any previous intimacy between God and the human. For Jesus is the revelation, the living message, of the Father, describing the inner life of Yahweh in every act he performs: "Philip . . . whoever has seen me has seen the Father" (Jn 14:9).[7]

Even this is not enough intimacy. For Jesus gives himself in the sacrament of the Eucharist so that he himself, the living fleshly covenant with the Father, would be continously present to us down through the centuries in an unforgettable way. Since the other six sacraments find their fulfillment in the Eucharist, Jesus would be with us as a chosen message of the Father in the key moments of our lives: birth, adolescence, sin, marriage, priesthood and death. What more could he do to repair the rupture of intimacy which is sin?

The "more" that Christ could do was to send the Holy Spirit to inform and thus reform his people into his image. Here the intimacy of the befriending (the advocate) Spirit would enable baptism to lift the people of God into the very life of the Trinity, would enable the sacrament of penance to repair the rupture of intimacy with the Trinity and between the members of the body of Christ, would enable confirmation to incorporate the people of God better into the Spirit's apostolic work, and would empower the Eucharist to bring all peoples into the body of Christ for the full intimacy of the Christ life.[8]

Clearly, then, revelation is the most intimate of divine acts and fittingly is the most powerful way of reconciling the people to God and to each other after they have ruptured this intimacy. Genesis points the way to intimate reconciliation,

Moses establishes the covenant of intimacy, the prophets show it to be a marriage covenant, and Christ becomes the living covenant in the flesh. As a result, the sacraments become the key moments of intimacy which seal the union of men with each other and with God in the mystical body of Christ.

3. The Sense of Sinfulness Is Not Prayerlessness

It may be high time to describe the prayer of admitted sinfulness and to show how it reveals a new stage of intimacy with Christ. We must, however, first emphasize how different is the sense of sinfulness from the state of prayerlessness. For, when a person, experiencing a deep sense of sinfulness, mistakes it for the state of prayerlessness, he or she can needlessly take on a crippling false guilt and a resultant depression. This makes all prayer unnecessarily difficult.

Put graphically and briefly, the state of prayerlessness is a believer's slow throttling of intimacy with God. It is a closing off of God from the deepest level of one's experience. One tries many maneuvers and clever tricks to hide this fact from oneself: "My work is my prayer" or "Others can do the praying while I bail out the boat" or "There'll be plenty of time to pray when I'm retired" or "I'm not the praying type" or "How can God ask me to do this type of job and still ask me to pray?" Such excuses lived for many years produce in the Christian a "terrible peace" but not the serenity of Christ.

Before diagnosing the state of prayerlessness, we must make two cautionary remarks: first, the prayerless person of whom we speak here is well balanced and not neurotic or psychotic; second, the characteristics etching his or her profile are chronic, not occasional as with all of us. The first characteristic of the believing prayerless person is heavy ennui manifested as a constant restlessness. The prayerless person wants everything and, when everything is had, feels more empty than ever—wandering from the television room to a drink or three in the kitchen, then to a lone drive in the car, next to a bar, and then finally back home to the silent

apartment. Second, this person experiences lonesomeness in
the midst of a party or in a conversation with a close friend;
the self is asking deep within: "What the hell am I doing
here?" The meaning of life seems to be draining out of mind
and heart.

There is, too, a chronic sense of distancing from those
with whom the prayerless person once shared so much in
work, talk, and ideals. There is even the beginning of hostility
toward them in cutting cynicism, in the sardonic grin, in the
cutting laugh which unnerves the surrounding people, in a
tight meanness so unlike the former relaxed self. Fourth, the
prayerless Christian experiences a sense of unreality about the
presence of Christ in the Eucharistic sacrifice (a hoary custom
finally unmasked), about the historical aspects of the Gospels
(who doesn't see the blatant contradictions?), about religious
people (why all the enthusiasm?), about religious vows
(sorority or fraternity for those over forty who can't make it in
the crazy world), about religion (does God care?—if he
exists). Then out of these attitudes comes the gradual
compromising which passes itself off as realistic honesty (why
shouldn't I get my share of the goodies before others grab
them off? I like nice things too).

This leads into the sixth characteristic of prayerlessness:
the manipulating mentality. Here the will of God turns cloudy
as the "political act" becomes paramount. This act provides a
better hold on the job one has, enables one to curry favor
with the group leader, improves one's image, puts the enemy
in an embarrassing position, assures one's safety even if the
security of others is jeopardized. Naturally this self-
centeredness renders the manipulator joyless so that he or she
feels envy, even dislike, for those who appear happy. The
latter's contentment, even amid sorrows and suffering, is more
than a surface irritation to the prayerless person; it is a
terrible challenge to his or her way of life (suppose I'm totally
wrong about what matters in life?).

This is the thumbnail sketch of the believing person with
the prayerless life. Recall that this is a chronic condition, not
merely an occasional feeling, of an otherwise balanced

personality. Here the prayerless person finally discovers that Christ is no longer real but only an historical shadow and that the resurrection is a communal delusion, a great hoax perpetrated on the gullible for the last twenty centuries of Christian misery. What is left for the prayerless person? Day-to-day living in which one grabs off the small chance pleasures and joys. Here is a life without faith "till death do us in."

4. Prayer of Sinfulness and the Sacraments

This portrait, exaggerated for the sake of clarity, enables one to contrast the state of prayerlessness sharply with the sense of sinfulness. Such contrast is important because a developed sense of one's sinfulness sets the prayer of admitted sinfulness into action. To see this, let us first define what is meant by the sense of sinfulness; it is the praying person's conviction that he or she is quite capable of committing any sin imaginable, unless God intervenes with his graceful strength.[9]

To illustrate this, let me recall a certain priest's experience during the years of dyspepsia, 1969–1970. With student rioting ringing in his ears, with eight out of his twenty-three fellow-ordained priests leaving the priesthood to marry, with the Church rattling around him from the percussion of Vatican II changes, with a new job to learn amid angry co-workers, with a new sense of his own fragility from having recently fallen in love, he is pacing up and down in the center aisle of a deserted, locked church and telling God how dark everything is. Suddenly at the back of the church, it strikes him like a lightning bolt that he is capable of just about any sin he has ever read about or imagined. His vulnerability is total; he feels like a lost soul.

In the midst of this interior devastation, he next realizes that, despite all his capability, he has not committed all of these scandalous sins. But why not? Because he has been carefully protected, delicately provided for. Just as suddenly as he has been made aware of his dark sinfulness, his easy slipping into any sin, he is now brightly aware that the Lord has lovingly protected him from his own drives, selfishness, meanness, and past sins. He now feels that he, the sinner, is affectionately held by the Lord. This love has been with him before he sinned, while he was sinning, and after he had sinned; it is the Lord's faithfulness to him.

A great sense of relief comes over the priest. He has finally joined the Church of fellow sinners and dropped off the burden of self-righteousness. A conviction has settled into his heart: he is lovable to God no matter what happens. Amid all the swirling changes of his world and Church, he has found his home, his center of the universe. For he is the Lord's man and no one else's. This sharp sense of sinfulness is worlds apart from the state of prayerlessness previously described. His conviction of sinfulness is filled with a peaceful sense of God's affectionate presence at the center of his being. He feels ready to do great things for the Lord.

This sense of sinfulness (with its almost simultaneous devastation and exultation) can now be lifted into the prayer of admitted sinfulness by the reconciling sacrament of penance or by the anointing sacrament of the sick. The sacrament of reconciliation does not merely lure me into facing my defects, failures, and past and present sins. It also encourages me to live honestly within them, i.e., not to be overwhelmed with a crippling guilt but to patiently accept their drag on any good I do.

For this reason, I tend to be more realistic in my expectations and in the execution of my decisions. For when I leave the place of my confession, I do not walk alone into my daily duties and problems—unless I want to. The Council of Trent assures the confessed sinner that actual graces (Christ presenting himself to us in our particular needs) happen through the days following upon one's reception of the sacrament of reconciliation. All this steadily promotes one's union with Christ, that is, one's prayer of admitted sinfulness.

Indeed, this sacrament paradoxically develops self-trust because in it Christ has entrusted me with himself and with his people whom I try to serve in the family, among dependents, amid clientele, and at the parish. Because of this entrusting, I find myself trying to develop the skills and talents needed to serve better these friends of God—out of gratitude for the Lord's forgiveness and faithfulness to me. There is a new confidence that I fit well into the Lord's kingdom. At this point, after surveying a series of conversions stretching back over my life, I now know that I dare never forget the prayer of admitted sinfulness. For it is what frees me from the burden of self-righteousness, enables me to live prudently within all my sin-baggage, reminds me of all the Lord has entrusted to me, and fills me with gratitude for the life God has given me.

In addition to the sacrament of reconciliation, the sacrament of the sick also vitalizes my prayer of admitted sinfulness. During sickness, in the midst of depression, there is both time and motivation to recall my life and to sound out the values knitting it together. Are these the values with which I would die peacefully? Or are they values which would seem tawdry under the piercing light of suffering and which would haunt me rather than cheer me at this moment? Can I seek forgiveness from the Lord without offering it to those who have hurt me?

Into this atmosphere the sacrament of the sick introduces Christ, the physician and therapist. As always he begins with the physical illness, touching the eyes dimmed with glaucoma, the leg withered by a stroke, the brain painfully tortured by tumor. Then he works to lift the depression of suffering by letting me know that not a twinge of pain is ever wasted by him, that this suffering is the price of an earthy wisdom gotten in no other way, that this suffering is not without its present and future joy as good friends unite to support me. At the spiritual level he asks whether I could have opened my heart to him and to others without this suffering and its sacrament. In other words, could I have seen suffering as the entrance into deeper intimacy with him and the sacrament as an invitation to never limit this intimacy offered by the crucified one? Could I, then, have recognized death as the beginning, not the end, of a fuller life?

Thus the sacrament of the sick is a walking within Christ's own passion. During it, worldliness gets burnt away by the flaming ultimate meaning of suffering: each of us uniquely reveals the extent and the quality of God's suffering in Christ. Further, within the devastation of Christ's and the Christian's sufferings, there lurks the hidden exaltation of the resurrection. This fills the sufferer with confident hope at the very time when others, much like Job's friends, come to comfort the sinful sufferer and end up distraught. Here the prayer of admitted sinfulness shows its depths of simultaneous sorrow and joy, passion and resurrection.

5. The Workings of the Prayer of Admitted Sinfulness

Though it is helpful to know the dynamics entering into the prayer of admitted sinfulness, still it may be more helpful to recognize just how this prayer works within us. First of all, it would seem to have two sides to it. Much like a tapestry, there is the ratty side of my person and of this prayer which makes me aware of all my weaknesses, inadequacies, past sins, and basic defects. It is not the pretty side of me or of my prayer. There are all those loose threads of my life to humiliate me regularly, to ground me in harsh reality. Nevertheless, these loose threads cannot be pulled at violently lest the other beautiful side of me and of my prayer be shredded.

The violent Mary Magdalene (seven devils had been cast out of her) and the violent John the apostle (he wanted to call down fire and brimstone on a Samaritan village for not welcoming the Lord) had to learn respect for themselves first in order to be reverent toward others later. Violence toward one's vices may well rip out one's gifts. Sensuality on one's ratty side may well be sensitivity to others on the beautiful side; harsh pride on the bad side could be singleness of purpose on the good side. The prayer of admitted sinfulness may teach a person, then, how to live patiently and wisely within shortcomings.

This prayer has its second and beautiful side. Thus, because a woman is deeply aware of her ratty side, because she is being freed from her false righteousness (typified by the Pharisee downgrading with his lofty prayers the poor publican in the back of the synagogue), she may find herself more trusting of others and more joyfully sensitive to their hopes and needs. Again, in her own felt helplessness, she may admit to the Lord, "Yes, it is your world, Lord, not mine, not Marx's, not Nietzsche's. Yes, this university at which I work is not mine, nor is it the conservatives' university, nor the liberals' nor the radicals'; it is yours, Lord—and now I can relax my gut a bit."

This woman may even recall Paul's lament: "I do not do what I want to do, but what I hate" (Rom 7:15). Or she may look to St. Augustine's discouragement at the snarled and broken threads of his interior life. For it produced the magnificent *Confessions* (cf. Book 10) where he shares the two-sided tapestry of his life with the only one who could knit him together, Christ. She might remember the Psalms 78 (7, 11, 42) and 106 (7, 13, 21) urging us never to forget our sins and God's gifts lest we become hardhearted toward God (and toward others?). She may discover that prayer of admitted sinfulness is a steady facing of death in the midst of good health, of suffering in the midst of joy, of loss in the midst of full trust, so that she may never become insensitive to life's losers, to the sick and to the dying. In fact, she may wonder whether the graceful liberty of a Francis of Assisi and of a Francis Xavier is not their supreme trust in a God who could love them in the midst of their sins and sinfulness, and in a Christ who could die brutally for them before they had ever admitted to a single sin (Rom 4:8–10).

Thus the prayer of admitted sinfulness is a prayer of stark honesty about one's sinfulness. But it also includes persistent trust in Christ's love for his sinful brother and sister and strong confidence in one's gifts, skills and hopes as promotive of Christ's kingdom. It is a prayer enspirited by the dual sacraments of reconciliation and of the sick as they instill the

confidence and wisdom necessary to be starkly honest, fully
trusting and hard working in Christ.

Actually prayer of admitted sinfulness is the safest
psssible prayer of all (and sometimes the richest) because it
knocks us off our towering, self-righteous perch, because it
produces solidarity or intimacy with our Church of sinners,
because it induces a gratitude rendering us zealous to serve
the marginal people of our society and to reunite them within
the Church, Christ's mystical body. This prayer, then, makes
us like the Alcoholics Anonymous. For they are continually
humiliated by their ever pressing weakness.[10] Often enough,
they are still not reunited with their families, yet they are
strongly supportive of others (out of their own weakness and
suffering) and are eager to see their own peace and joy
reproduced in others.

This prayer of admitted sinfulness is a rough and tough
form of intimacy. Yet as Van Breemen has noted acutely:
mission starts with remission.[11] We enter into the lives of
others gracefully only after we have finally learned to live
gracefully in our own lives precisely through such suffering of
ourselves. What better preparation for the life of intimacy
with God and with others and what more realistic entrance
into the hard work of building Christ's kingdom than the
prayer of admitted sinfulness! The next chapter will try to
demonstrate that this is a true paradox, not simple foolishness.

Stage Five
The Prayerful "More":
Daring Intimacy Within Apostolic Work[1]

Why do some zealous workers for the Lord burn out so swiftly? Indeed, there is one type of "burn-out," the super-apostle,[2] whose career is especially puzzling. He or she enters the Christian arena with such energy, inventiveness, and hope, works so ferociously, challenges so vociferously, suddenly goes dead so disastrously.[3] Such instances of "burn-out" reveal four stages in their rocket careers. First, there is a gradual abandonment of prayer in their fervent busyness. Second, in not admitting their own limitations, they find themselves refusing to accept the limitations of others. Third, in not putting aside time to become sensitive to their own selves (to their own needs, emotional states, compulsions, and motives), they lose sensitivity to other people's wants, ideas, feelings, drives and desires. Fourth, their physical and psychological exhaustion affects their faith-life deeply so that, out of desperate frustration, they are tempted (and sometimes yield) to a reversal of their life values: from working with the poor to cultivating the rich, from raising social issues to pursuing individual career-success, from single-mindedness to double-standard dealings, and sometimes even from faith to agnosticism. Few of them ever return to their former work. This is the super-apostle type of "burn out."[4]

Ironically, such "burnouts" have very likely failed to find the apostolic prayer of the "more." For this type of prayer enables the praying person to live peacefully within limitations, to accept the frustrations coming from intimacy with people and to discover the intimacy offered by God within apostolic work. It also includes a quiet underlying joy which is both strength and stability. Does all this seem like a facile judgment foisted upon broken apostles who, having

53

suffered much for God's people, deserve a more generous
view? If this judgment does seem an overly facile
interpretation of a much more complex phenomenon, then let
us explore a spiritual movement directly opposed to the
super-apostle's failure in accepting limitations and in being
sufficiently sensitive to self and others.

1. Sensitizing the Self to God and to Others

In traditional manuals of spirituality, purification of the
self was emphasized. Nowadays it is translated as sensitizing
the self to its limitations, then accepting them, next living
prudently within their boundaries, and finally discovering the
joy of the "more" within them. One could say that these four
steps are a gritty way of moving toward intimacy with
oneself—a movement directly opposite to the super-apostle's
second and third stages.

Of these four steps toward self-intimacy, the first is to
recognize one's limitations in some depth. But such
recognition takes a long time since one has to undergo
numerous successes and failures before one has enough data
to spot the patterns of limitation and to observe that they are
present in almost every act one performs. For example, if I
suffer from vanity, this defect does not allow me to admit my
limitations very easily. I have to witness my vanity demanding
(1) that people give me top billing in any endeavor, (2) that
everybody but myself gets blamed for a cooperative failure,
(3) that lavish praise be used to galvanize me into action, and
(4) that others become rungs on my ladder to success. In
other words, I have to observe that the weight of my vanity is
crushing out my health, my once daring inventiveness (I don't
dare lose), my love for anyone else but myself—before I will
admit to its presence in me.

If I should eventually recognize the devastating effects of
vanity on myself, my work, and my comrades, then the second
step is to accept these limitations.[5] But what is this
acceptance? Is it simply a surrendering to my limitation ("So,
I'm vain; that's the way I am and people better get used to

it")? Or is acceptance a clever masking of my vanity with
polite strategies (e.g., high praise and special gifts for those
who "cooperate nicely") in order to secure what I want? Or is
acceptance saying to God: "Lord, I don't like this limitation of
being a vain peacock; it embarrasses me often but I'll try to
live with it and not give up using my talents as best I can"?
Usually this last type of acceptance occurs only after I have
unsuccessfully tried to get rid of my limitation by violent
action. For when I tried to pull out the threads on the ugly
side of my tapestry-personality, I discovered that I had
loosened and disarrayed the threads on the beautiful side.
Thus as I attempted desperately to overcome my vanity with
public self-humiliations I ruined my natural vivacity.

Once I admit, like Augustine, that to be a creature is not
to be God but is to have limitations, and once I discover that I
will be enjoying these inadequacies as I fall into the grave,
then a new realism is born in me. I come to accept that my
limitations are the other side of my gifts (my laziness may well
be part of my contemplative stance; my sensuality may also be
related to my sensitivity to beauty). Thus both gifts and
inadequacies are not to be rooted out but to be lived within.

But how does one live within limitations? The third step
toward sensitizing myself to God and to others is to give up
the useless lamenting of my faults and to learn how to balance
my weaknesses with my strengths so that the weaknesses do
not disrupt my projects. I am not receiving the praise I
deserve for my work with the Teens' Club. But I do not let
this totally dampen my enthusiasm for the Club's next outing.
Indeed, I even manage to praise the young Club president for
his latest coup, a successful gym party. But vanity is not easy
to live with and so I cannot resist mentioning that he could
have done a better job of cleaning up the gym after the event.
Such vanity continues to plague a person because, through
the new sensitivity to it, the vain person discovers it in ever
new places and ways. This produces dark periods of
discouragement which only conversation with a close friend
and God can brighten.

As a result, the fourth step of achieving sensitivity toward self and others (and thus of reaching self-intimacy) is getting accustomed to a sense of helplessness. This is the feeling of being unable to cope with one's limitations in a very difficult situation. In this less-than-pleasant experience, one becomes aware that without God one is helpless and that God is truly one's savior, one's rescuer. A person has a sense here of being leveled by God and by circumstances.

Yet precisely at this point one feels a new sense of solidarity with the Lord's marginal people (the anawim): the born losers, the desperate ones, the little ones, the Church of sinners. One feels, then, much less capable of making harsh judgments on them—if only for fear that one's judgment may be on oneself. In addition, one experiences a strange quiet joy in the depths of the self because one is being liberated from vanity; and in the new relaxed feeling, one gradually becomes aware of the "more" in one's work and prayer. To see how apostolic work and prayer reveal the "more" (God's presence dimly perceived), let us glance at these two aspects of Christian living separately, if that be possible.

2. The "More" in the Experience of Apostolic Work

If the "more" is the Lord acting through, and therefore intimately present to, the experience of the apostolic worker, how does one experience this "more"? Response: by observing how the results of one's work far exceed one's potential—a potential accurately known through one's prayer of sinfulness and through living within one's limitations in a sense of helplessness. As St. Paul has noted: "I willingly boast of my weaknesses that the power of Christ may rest upon me . . . for when I am powerless, it is then that I am strong" (2 Cor 12:9–10). A priest of my acquaintance, who prepares his homilies with some care and is gifted with inventiveness, told me that on two or three occasions he had tried to construct a homily, found himself with no insights, decided to tell the congregation that he had no homily, went out to the altar to sit for the scriptural readings, suddenly found a homily

forming within him, gave the homily and recognized it as
much better than usual, received some glowing compliments
for it, and was able to say mysteriously to the complimenter:
"Thank you, but that was not my homily."

Another person who has been writing articles and books
for close to thirty years told me of his experience. He had
taken antibiotics to combat influenza which kept returning
through the month of March. One night, filled with
medication, he awoke at 3 A.M. with thirteen logically knit
ideas for a book on university education. He got up, lurched
over to his desk, wrote down the thirteen in twenty minutes,
went back to bed and slept another six hours. That morning,
after a cup of coffee, he went to his desk to read the thirteen
ideas for a good laugh much needed. To his surprise, their
conciseness and their logic held up in the bright daylight; and
he wrote in two more ideas. When Easter vacation came, he
spent ten days outlining these ideas into fifteen chapters
through sixty-five pages of manuscript.

Then during the summer, he wrote for eighty straight
days, six to seven hours per day, and finished a first rough
draft of eleven chapters. He thought that he would be
exhausted when the September university classes began right
after the eighty days of writing; instead, he was as relaxed as
though he had just come from a vacation, and this state
perdured through the school year. Later, the remaining four
chapters took him twelve months to write. But his experience
was of writing far beyond himself not simply in endurance,
but also in richness of content, in tight organization of ideas,
in a certain depth of wisdom, and in the joy of his work. He
thinks of this as the "more" of Christ in his work; never
before or since has he had a similar experience. He is
convinced that he was not working alone during this project.

Another person has spoken to me of this experience of
the "more" in her giving of spiritual direction to others.
Though a veteran in this work, she is often surprised at the
wise advice she gives, at the question she asks which unlooses
a flood of memories in the directee, at the comment made
which the directee learns to treasure as a lifelong directing

influence. She thinks of this as the "X factor," the Holy Spirit, entering into her advice, question, or comment to enrich each far beyond the director's knowledge or intent. I would suspect that the father or mother has had a similar experience in correcting children, in plotting mortgage payments, in resolving family conflicts, and in learning to meet the needs and hopes of the spouse.

These examples of how the "more" may be experienced in apostolic work indicate the intimacy with which God works within these persons' limitations to empower their labors beyond their realistic expectations. Of course, the "more" becomes recognizable since these people know well their inadequacies, have accepted them and lived within them for years. Who experiences the helplessness of personal limitations more acutely than the parents of three teenagers as they try to guide the youngsters into adulthood amid the thousand and one traps seductively laid out for the unwary? And so, who can better recognize the "more" in their experience?

Besides experiencing the "more" in the unexpectedly greater-than-usual results of daily tasks, one can sharpen awareness of the "more" through what may be called the "stretch." This is the spending of one's energies on behalf of Christ's people in order to make room for the "more" of Christ's intimacy in them and in oneself. The risk involved in the "stretch" is not some imprudent extravagance. It is, for example, trying to work with people whom some years ago one had found quite difficult, e.g., the elderly or teenagers or working mothers. Or it is endeavoring to counsel people at new depth in their problems and sorrows, that is, with the follow-through of telephone calls, visits, and remembrances. Or it is stretching one's capacities with new knowledge (e.g., reentering college to acquire new helping skills) or with a new type of work (moving from role of secretary to that of home-maker) or with a new housing arrangement (becoming court-appointed guardians for children from broken families) or with a new language (for teaching Hispanics).[6] All this "stretch" makes room for new intimacy with self, others, and

God because it is meant to extend more help to God's family so that this family can enjoy a fuller life with Christ.

In all of this there can be a quiet sustaining joy—an alluring hope. For the sacraments of baptism and confirmation support such stretching. Thus baptism commits one to meet the needs of the family of God and promises the worker that the indwelling Trinity accompanies him or her in all the dangers and sufferings of such service. Confirmation is a deeper rooting of the same commitment and a further strengthening of the mandate from Christ: "Make disciples of all the nations. Baptize them in the name of the Father, and of the Son, and of the Holy Spirit. Teach them to carry out everything I have commanded you. And know that I am with you always, until the end of the world" (Mt 28:19–20).

Even the sacrament of the sick enters into the apostolic "more" of both work and prayer. For the sacrament is meant to restore physical health so that one can again serve the Christian community or anyone else who needs assistance. It also teaches us to prize not only physical health but also psychological balance, not only one's work but also one's friendships, not only one's friends but also one's acquaintances, co-workers, and the very people served by one's skill of nursing or car-repair or entertaining or counseling or mail-delivering. Out of this return to health, to mental balance, and to renewed sense of dedication can come a new intimacy with friends, co-workers, clientele, self, and God. This would show itself in a restored hope in these people, in a new sense of the worthwhileness of one's work, and in a deeply pervasive joy of accomplishment.

Lastly, this experience of the workaday "more" is deepened when one gradually learns to give up the need to have total control over one's work, when one allows the "divine more" to do some of the worrying and planning. Such trust lets events and other people be; it does not try to take over each situation and each person so that nothing can possibly go wrong. Here one has the opportunity to watch how the "more" conducts affairs after one has done everything possible to make an event fruitful but has also let

the Lord do some of the worrying and exercise some control
(rather than oneself taking desperate measures to insure
success). Christ himself did just this during the three
temptations. He rejected the attractive strategies of Satan for
building the kingdom (fascinate the multitudes with miracles
for power, use the Roman Empire for prestige, and adapt the
Jewish church presumptuously to his new Church—Lk 4:1–
13). He let his Father set the strategy, namely, to visit each
small town, to evangelize it, to cure each person one by one,
and to follow through with individual conversations.

Christ also "stretched" himself to the limit in constant
journeying, in sketching out the kingdom with paradoxical
beatitudes, in tense battling with the Pharisees and Saduccees,
and in later asking people to be ready to eat his flesh and to
drink his blood ("From this time on, many of his disciples
broke away and would not remain in his company any
longer"—Jn 6:66). Christ well knew the experience of the
surprising "more" in his apostolic work. After hearing the
pagan centurion's description of his divine authority, Christ
expresses amazement to his disciples: "I have never found this
much faith in Israel" (Mt 8:10). He recognized the "more"
because his desert experience had taught him his own human
limits. Yet he gambled with the "stretch" throughout his
public life so that at the end he was stretched out to the
ultimate. For he had given up all his controls to the Father in
total trust. No wonder, then, that the Lord Jesus offered us
the sacraments of baptism, confirmation and anointing of the
sick to strengthen us for the "stretch." This would deepen
our trust in himself and in the Father so that we could better
know the "more" in our prayer and work.

3. Five Characteristics of the "More" in Apostolic Prayer

After one has prayed faithfully over a good number of
years, a new type of prayer develops, one that often
scandalizes the praying person. The latter wonders whether
he or she has failed the Lord in some basic way, whether he
or she has lost the ability to pray, whether the Lord has lost

interest and perhaps may be abandoning him or her. This is not the state of prayerlessness though it bears some resemblances to the latter. Therefore, the person undergoing this new type of prayer needs to be reassured that all is not lost. Rather, a new depth of intimacy is opening up. Basically, in the state of prayerlessness, the person has lost interest in God, while in this new prayer of the apostolic "more" the praying person thinks God has lost interest in him or her. But the praying person's very concern indicates strong interest in God—unlike the unconcern of the prayerless person.

The "more" of apostolic prayer reveals God's presence in five paradoxical ways or characteristics. The first is a seeming emptiness in the person's one-to-one prayer with the Lord— no insights, no consolations, no sense of progress or growth, but, instead, a feeling of stagnation and of apparent boredom. The prayer comes down to simply presenting oneself to the Lord. For all the points of prayer-focus such as a Scripture passage or a bit of spiritual reading or a fear or some hope yield nothing. The paradox arises when, despite this emptiness, the praying person experiences a strange sense of worthwhileness upon completion of the prayer. Something has happened deep down in the person but it is not describable to anyone. This makes it quite different from the state of prayerlessness.

A second paradoxical feature of this prayer is that it feels directionless—often because the prayer is not moving according to one's accustomed way or according to one's previous plans. Nor usually is the person's apostolic work moving predictably. But underneath the turmoil there is a serene patience with God and with co-workers. It is as if the praying person did not care about the final outcome of the work even though he or she is working as hard and as methodically as before. Again, paradoxically, the praying person, though feeling blind, suspects that this is the right road and that, on looking back much later, he or she will recognize the direction as right.

Of course, from the previous two characteristics, one would deduce the third: a sense of helplessness, especially if one is meeting some heavy opposition in one's work or is suddenly hit with unexpected illness. Yet, paradoxically, within this experience there is a strong hope that things will work out so long as one stays loyal to fellow workers and to those served by the work. Consequently, this praying person wonders at his or her own lack of discouragement when meeting depressed colleagues.

All this leads to the fourth feature of apostolic prayer of the "more": God's seeming absence from one's prayer. Again, however, God paradoxically erupts into one's workday in new ways. For example, one experiences a sharper sense of divine providence when events dovetail to achieve an unexpected result such as a chance airport-meeting with a long-lost friend of high school days. Or one glimpses with shocking clarity the lovable nobility of a co-worker's ordinary act of generosity. Or sometimes there is a felt sense of God operating within one for just a brief moment at the most hectic part of the day. Or during one's desert prayer God momentarily seems to give an affectionate touch like the parent patting the head of the child to let the child know that all is quite well between them. Because something not calculable by usual standards is happening, this veteran of prayer would not think of giving up on prayer even though he or she may occasionally shorten it in sheer frustration. The one-to-oneness, the satisfying co-presence of God and self, is somehow there although in a more obscure, groping way.

The fifth characteristic of this apostolic prayer of the subjective "more" is its frequent reversal of the objective "more" found in apostolic work. In a mysterious way, at one time an awful failure in one's apostolic work will be accompanied by a prayer filled with serene joy. At another time, however, a rich experience of work accomplished beautifully will contrast sharply with a deeply felt emptiness and restlessness in one's prayer. But this seesaw experience, though paradoxical, does not discourage the praying person. For it is the same one-to-one presence with the Lord in work and in prayer despite diversity of feelings.[7]

But then what is the profile which these five characteristics of the prayer of the apostolic "more" reveal to us? As one might expect, this prayer consists mainly in recognizing, enjoying, and giving thanks for the merely occasional appearances, yet persistent presence, of the "more" in one's work and prayer. This presence is recognized in the unexpectedly greater results of one's work or prayer, in the "stretch," and in the refusal to attempt total control of the situation. In this prayer, amid seeming emptiness, lack of direction, helplessness, absence of God, and reversals of feeling, there is an enduring patience, a strong hope, a sense of worthwhileness and a half-glimpsed joy. In elderly people who have faithfully prayed to God for others amid difficult tasks, we find this prayer remarkably strong. For they know intimately who is the power, the wisdom and the secret joy in their living.

4. Paradoxical Presence of the "More" in One's Emptiness

Thus at the very moment when one's work and prayer feel totally empty, one can best experience the "more" in them. For the sharper the pain of my poverty, the stronger can be the sense of the "more" in it. At this stage of life I can discover God doing great things through my helplessness, working efficiently and intelligently through my bewildering limitations along with my co-workers and our situation. But why does God wait so long to show himself and why act so hiddenly? Because he must be sure that I thoroughly know my limitations and emptiness lest I foolishly mistake his power for my own. The better I know my inadequacies, the more clearly I see and the more deeply I appreciate the extent of his power working within my limited prayer and apostolate.

Because the "more" in my prayer- or work-experience is clearly indicated by results qualitatively exceeding my efforts, I find myself with a deepened empathy for the shortcomings, emotional upsets, and sufferings of others since I can no longer self-righteously think of myself as the self-made woman or man. For this reason I am more fit for spiritual direction, for apostolic cooperation, and for family living. Then, too, this experience strips me down to the simple desire to find and to do God's preferences rather than my own. This is to delight God by doing exactly what he wants, when and where he wants it. Now I am more fully ready to discern God's will. Here, again, deep satisfaction is felt in direct contrast with the simultaneous pain.

As Thomas Green has noted in *Darkness in the Marketplace*, the sense of helplessness in one's apostolic work is parallel to, even compenetrated with, the passivity in one's prayer. For the praying person is being sensitized not only to the self and to fellow creatures but also to God himself. The praying person finds the self lured again and again into the desert experience of one-to-one prayer and wonders what the lure can be if it is not the "more." Amid avalanches of distractions or amid the dry winds of seeming boredom, one nevertheless feels a certain worthwhileness in the experience—perhaps a subtle joy? This is not to deny that at times the "more" of apostolic prayer can be profoundly joyful, deeply serene, and exuberant with life.[8] But at this particular stage of intimacy now being described, the "more" is very likely a zone of quiet in one's prayer experience.

5. Christ Trains His Apostles for the "More"

If one is wondering whether the above account of the "more" in apostolic prayer and work is valid, then one should note how Christ trained his apostles and disciples. He seems to have been aiming to develop the bond of intimacy among them and then between them and him. This intimacy bond would later unify his people as a Church. Why else, in John the evangelist's account of the Last Supper, would he speak to his disciples of the Triune God indwelling in each person (Jn 14:16–20) and forming such persons into an intimate unity with the Trinity (17:20–23)? Why else would Christ inspire the apostle Paul to call the Church the mystical body of Christ?

To understand the "more" of apostolic work and prayer and to see its close connection with the intimacy bond among the apostles and with Christ, note that he first sends the apostles out in twosomes of total vulnerability: "Take nothing for the journey, neither walking staff nor traveling bag; no bread, no money. No one is to have two coats. Stay at whatever house you enter" (Lk 9:3–4). Thus the two apostles would have to lean on each other for support and be very dependent precisely on those whom they were to evangelize and heal. The situation was, as it were, rigged for intimacy. When the apostles reported back to Christ, they expressed surprise at all they had accomplished (the objective "more"). But immediately afterward they were asked to pass out the five loaves and two fishes *before* the latter had been completely multiplied. No small trust was demanded here in the subjective "more," namely, the Father.

Nevertheless, during this period, the apostles wanted power more than trust. Right after Jesus' second prediction of his passion, death, and resurrection, they were busy discussing who among them was the greatest (Lk 9:44–46) and John the apostle was ready to stop the man expelling demons in Jesus' name because he was not of their number (Lk 9:49–50). Indeed, John and James were glad to call down fire on an inhospitable Samaritan village (Lk 9:53–54) and to back up their mother's request that they sit on Jesus' right and left in the kingdom lest they miss out during the brokerage of power (Mt 20:20–28). It was going to take some time before the apostles would learn to live in trust of the "more" and not to try to control all things.

Meanwhile, using the same strategy as with the apostles, Jesus was sending the seventy-two disciples out like "lambs in the midst of wolves" stripped of protecting staff, sandals, amenities of greeting, and choice of hospitality (Lk 10:3–7). But the vulnerable ones, having learned to live trustingly with the assigned partner and with any welcoming family of the village, are astounded at (the "more") their power over the demons. Nevertheless they are advised to rejoice not so much in the subjection of the devils to them (the objective results of the "more") as in the inscription of their names in heaven (Lk 10:17-20). Friendship with the "more" is of far greater importance than the experience of the "more," God's power exercised through the disciples' vulnerability.

Earlier, Jesus had honestly described to his followers how out-of-control is the Christian's life and work. After sketching the revolutionary values of the kingdom (the beatitudes) in the conservative Jewish society, he instructs them to love their enemies, to bless those who curse them, to turn the other cheek, to give not only the requested coat but the unrequested shirt, to be compassionate like the heavenly Father (Lk 6:17-36). "If the smallest things are beyond your power, why be anxious about the rest?" (Lk 12:26), he asks. But Jesus reassures not merely his first century disciples when he says, "Everything has been given over to me by my Father. No one knows the Son except the Father and no one knows the Father except the Son—and anyone to whom the Son wishes to reveal him" (Lk 10:22). So, the intimacy between Father and Son, shared with the disciples and us, is the source of the power within us; it is the "more" which consolingly enables us to pray and work beyond our limitations when the situation seems wild and out of control. This is what the disciples, like us, were being trained to recognize, accept and live.

There is a second important element in Christ's training of his disciples. It is the constant tension of the "stretch" in Jesus' life and consequently in their lives. Jesus admits to his disciples, "I have come to light a fire on the earth. How I wish the blaze were ignited! I have a baptism to receive. What anguish I feel till it is over! Do you think I have come to establish peace on the earth? I assure you, the contrary is true; I have come for division. From now on, a household of five will be divided three against two and two against three" (Lk 12:49-52). This "stretch" will reach its final tautness when he and his apostles cross the Kedron Valley on their way to Gethsemane's bloody sweat and Jesus remarks, "My heart is filled with sorrow to the point of death" (Mk 14:34; cf. Mt 26:38).

But this agony is simply the culmination of many previous tense times. There is the tension of the constant "stretch" as Jesus faces his own townspeople and turns them into potential murderers by warning that the Messiah may pass them by and that they risk no longer being considered the chosen people (Lk 4:14-30). Tension is tight, too, when he confronts the Pharisees and doctors of the law from all over Judea and even Jerusalem with his forgiveness of the paralytic's sins (Lk 5:17-26). Tension is in his shock at the Pharisees' inhumaneness when they scold his hungry disciples for shucking a few grain heads on the sabbath (Lk 6:1-5). The stretch of tension is in his exasperation at the Pharisees who set him up for a sabbath violation by putting a man with a withered hand toward the center of the synagogue gathering (Lk 6:6-11). So great is the exhausting stretch of his tension that during a storm he can sleep in a wildly tossing small boat and not hear the desperate shouting of his fisherman disciples (Lk 8:22-25). Even when Christ and the apostles try a little excursion across the lake for a quick rest, their nerves are stretched taut by the Gerasene demoniac's frenzied approach as soon as they set foot on the beach (Lk 8:26-39). Then, too, there is always Herod prowling about in the background (Lk 9:7-9).

Yet out of this tension and its stretching of nerves comes intimacy between the apostles and with Jesus. For Jesus caps his training with this upper-room remark after the resurrection: "Peace be with you. As the Father has sent me [vulnerable and stretching amid tension], so I send you. . . . Receive the Holy Spirit [the bond of intimacy]" (Jn 20:21-22). For he had earlier promised the disciples: "How much more will the heavenly Father give the Holy Spirit to those who ask him" (Lk 11:13). Amid the tense stretching of their lives, the disciples will experience the power of the Holy Spirit, the divine "more," in all their work and prayer. The Holy Spirit henceforth becomes the indwelling trainer of the disciples, their secret joy and strength, their direction-finder, their sense of worthwhileness, their serene hope, their unity of work and prayer.

6. A Risky Conclusion

Apostolic prayer of the "more" is an earthy prayer. Out of the rich loam of the prayer of sinfulness (which is a profound awareness of one's limitations and sins amid God's love) comes the prayer and work of the apostolic "more" for the recognition, acceptance and exploitation of these weaknesses. "Mission starts with remission," notes Van Breemen. The Lord's strategy is strange. One is expected to find intimacy, first with Christ and then with co-workers and with those one serves, precisely through the "stretch" of apostolic daring in new projects, new ways of doing things, new perils to oneself and to one's people.[9]

The prayer of the apostolic "more," then, is risky. It strips away pretensions. Next it demands that one carry the daily tensions of the "stretch" amid interior dryness and exterior challenges. Further, it requires that one daringly leave room for the "more" in one's work lest, in trying to exercise total control, one squeeze the "more" out of one's work and then wonder why the work has become a walk through trackless sand and is filled with the desert winds of vanity. Against this background, the "more" of the Holy Spirit will be recognizable as he empowers modern-day disciples to do deeds beyond their talents and amid their failings and with greater than expected results (sometimes with other than expected results). Thus the disciple, often unknowingly, is being invited to a deeper level of intimacy with the Lord where lies a quiet persistent joy.

This is the incredible mystery of the prayer of apostolic "more." Only faith and the tension of the "stretch" will reveal the Holy Spirit praying within us—admittedly with unutterable groanings (Rom 8:26) but also with the promised joy of truth and justice (Jn 14:16, 26; 16:7–15). In this way one is not burnt out by the fires of frustrated ambition but rather is warmed, illuminated and energized by the fire of the Spirit.

Stage Six
Prayer of Powerlessness:
Deep Intimacy of Marriage, Friendship
and Religious Vowed Life in Family of God[1]

The Lord speaks strangely as Gideon, his Israelite general, faces the hostile forces of Midian: "You have too many soldiers with you for me to deliver Midian into their power, lest Israel vaunt itself against me and say, 'My own power brought me the victory'" (Jgs 7:2). Therefore Gideon is instructed to cut his forces down to three hundred men so that it is clear that the victory is solely the work of Yahweh and not the victory of the Israelite soldiers. It should be noted, however, that Gideon is encouraged to use natural means for victory such as preliminary testing for the best fighters, a night attack, the blowing of trumpets, and the breaking of jars to suddenly reveal hidden torchlights (Jgs 7:4–22). Although the Israelite soldiery are made to feel their helplessness, they are still expected to use their intelligence, courage, and all previous military experience.

The paradox suffusing the whole scene is that in their powerlessness, God will operate powerfully if they do all in their own power to use the natural means at hand. (This reminds one of a reputed Ignatian dictum: pray as though all depended on prayer and work as though all depended on work.) Such teamwork, because of dire circumstances, should produce a camaraderie of intimacy between Gideon and God and between them and the three hundred soldiers. This trusting camaraderie, in turn, could be the source of the prayer of powerlessness.

But how does one begin to deal with this powerless state of mind and heart in its mysterious unifying of God and us? Should we first risk a description of the prayer of powerlessness so that we can focus attention on its essential

characteristics and at the same time challenge its "truth" with
our experiences? Could the prayer of powerlessness be
described as the discovering, reverencing, and promoting of
God's intimate mediation between spouses, between friends,
and between vowed religious amid fearsome perils—a
mediation that works most powerfully in their powerlessness,
that is, in their lack of control over events?

This daring type of prayer would be expected to open the
praying person, in turn, to a more intense and also richer
family-, neighborhood-, and God-life. If this should be the
case, then knowledge of the prayer of powerlessness would be
invaluable, especially if it were to reveal deeper stages of
intimacy with God and others. To assure realism, however, as
we appraise intimacy within the prayer of powerlessness, let
us first consider the perils of intimacy in marriage, friendship,
and religious vowed life.

1. The Perils of Intimacy Amid Daily Powerlessness

The romanticizing of marital intimacy has hardly
prepared the young newlyweds for the perils of intimacy.
After the first passionate months, they gradually discover how
arduous can be twenty-four-hours-per-day companionship,
even if they are both going off to different jobs after
breakfast. Neither has ever co-planned a single future with
another (future housing, children, financing, and education).
Neither has spent almost all his or her leisure with one other
person (what if both do not have the same liking for friends,
music, sports, reading, home repair?). Neither has ever had to
discover, suffer, understand, and share another's failings,
shortcomings, fears, and hopes as thoroughly, as tenderly, as
deeply as now. Friends can get away from each other or can
temporarily dodge the other's inadequacies, but not the
married in their fifty years of evenings together.

Then, too, there is the so-called "package choice" of the
in-laws. One does not merely marry the spouse; one also
willy-nilly marries his or her relatives "for better or for
worse." And the coming of the children is not unlike the

grand lottery. The future parent asks: "Will I like them? Will they like me? What will they become—and then do to us and for us?" The intimacy of marriage, though beautiful and rewarding, has a few perils.

Yet out of all this powerlessness, this lack of control over events (while the couple faces twenty-four hour companionship, the in-laws, the children and a co-future), intimacy can nevertheless rise with spouse, children, and relatives. In fact, such intimacy can act as a direct intimate contact with God. St. Paul (Eph 5:22–33) notes this when he uses marital intimacy as the model for the individual person's union with God. In a mysterious way, one union reveals the other, one intimacy promotes the other, one suffering-joying saves the other. A priest once related to me how his companioning of a sister-in-law during her fatal struggle with leukemia led to a deep intimacy with her which not only led him more deeply into his brother's life but also more fully into life with Christ. It was as though, between the three of them and God, there was for a while only one intimacy.

Friendship, too, is not without its perils of intimacy. It is quite possible to let a friendship die off. One or both friends can become very busy with career or marriage; a friend can move away to a distant part of the country and become preoccupied with new acquaintances, new jobs, new leisure pursuits like backpacking or theatre. Sometimes one of the friends experiences failure in job or marriage or self-worth (depression and psychiatric counseling can be quite introvertive). As someone has remarked, only the successful show up for reminiscence meetings and class reunions. Because of these events, friendship demands patience with each other's ups and downs and requires follow-through of letters, telephone calls, hospital visits, and leisure times together. This careful attentiveness is especially needed when one of the friends is undergoing a siege of illnesses with consequent loneliness or is enduring psychological trauma.

There is another complicating factor. As friends mature, they discover differing religious, political, and moral values. Here patience of the heart must bridge with acts of trust the intellectual chasms and the obstructive counter-convictions. This is costly in emotional stress. For in a long-time friendship of depth there is an implicit vow of "forever," and this vow, in times of distress, can be resented as a clamp on one's freedom.[2] This hits hardest those who are supporting other communities in addition to the friendship. Where does one find time to fulfill all one's obligations to the people intimate to one's life? At this time the thoughtful friend can feel helpless.

Yet out of all this powerlessness to cope with the intricacies of modern day friendship can come intimacy with God. For in the more thoughtful moments one can feel gratitude to God for the richness of friendships in one's life. At a business failure or in a hospital room or during a familiar birthday celebration, a person can experience the strengthening loyalty of friends and know intimately their inestimable value. In fact, often the very perils of intimate friendship reveal its beauty amid the ugliness of sickness or career failure or bitter family bickering.[3]

Not only marriage and friendship suffer the perils of intimacy. The vowed life of religious has its own set of dangers. The vows of religious certainly are made first and principally to God but they are also made to the community; one does marry the community. So, like the married person, the vowed religious can say, "If I'd ever known what I was getting into, I'd have. . . After all, I not only got into a lot of simultaneous blind dates, I married them all for better or for worse." But the blind dates could reply, "What you say is true, Buster (or Betty), but remember that you've made some great friends in the bargain and that you were one big blind date for all of us, too." Yes, religious life is especially rich in the opportunities for friendship because so much is done together for similar values and hopes, so much is suffered together in work and prayer, so much is enjoyed together in times of fun and even of tiredness.

Yet togetherness can also point to the perils of religious vowed life. Within the friendly confines of religious community, persons can always set up their own self-centered

kingdom of career, leisure companions, housing, and
economic independence so that they can live the life of the
self-satisfied bachelor or spinster. Then, too, the sweaty,
painful apostolic work can be dodged within the protective
community so that individuals can become slothful and
irresponsible both to their fellow religious and to those whom
they have been called to serve. These so-called religious can
eventually become high-class Pharisees because, underneath
their ostensibly dedicated life of vows, of community sharing,
and of apostolic endeavors, there lurks persistent vow-
cheating, individualism, and self-centered laziness. Nor do
they recognize that this very comfortable life is a perilous
hazard to their salvation, a betrayal of their community and a
grave dereliction of duty toward the people dependent on
their work. Rather it is taken as a right, even as a beautifully
humane way of living.

Out of these perils of intimacy in the religious life,
however, can come a type of intimacy which is like marriage
in its vowed life together and like friendship in its
spontaneous loyalty. Still this life has its own type of
intimacy—the intimacy of a fraternal or sisterly teamwork
aimed toward a common goal of serving school or parish or
publishing house or social agency or missionary endeavor.
This teamwork issues out of a common explicit pursuit of God
through work, liturgy, leisure and prayer. In such a situation,
lasting friendships naturally spring up to reinforce the shared
work and prayer—with an intimacy which reveals God and
thus goes far beyond apostolic teamwork.

Indeed, the gradual discovery of God in prayer reveals a
type and depth of friendship beyond the human and yet
enriching it. No human friend could ask what God asks; no
human friend could reply so deftly, so faithfully, so
passionately to one's love as God does. No human friendship
can render one so independent of, and yet so dependent on,
all other friendships that Christ can demand: "Be
compassionate, as your Father is compassionate" (Lk 6:36). As
in marriage and friendship, however, one is quite helpless to
control vowed religious life; it, too, has its ups and downs, its

unpredictable and frightening turns in the road, its cold and
hot days, its laughs and sharp conflicts, its loyalties and
betrayals.

What becomes clear after surveying the perils of intimacy
in marriage, friendship and vowed religious life, is (1) that the
intimacy is well worth the perils, (2) that intimacy can be very
revealing and therefore quite humiliating in its demands, (3)
that the perils of intimacy show us how powerless we are in
the most intimate, most rewarding moments of our lives. Yet
this powerlessness, this lack of control over events, can render
the spouse, the friend and the fellow religious even more
lovable as they look to us, their rescuers, for help. For we
witness here their noble struggle to stay open, trusting, and
peaceful amid the perils. And the sometimes powerlessness of
the supposed rescuer can bring him or her to call upon the
Lord for help and thus to experience the Lord working
through the caller's very weakness to accomplish the rescue.
Out of this mutual triangular dependence comes the
tenderness of intimacy, its tough perseverance in promoting
the beloved's life, and its hope in the goodness of God and of
neighbor.

But all this data does nothing if not raise two difficult
questions: (1) Precisely how does the sense of powerlessness
feel in such prayer? (2) How does such powerlessness in
Gospel personages and in life-situations reveal the meaning of
the prayer of powerlessness? Let us face the first of these two
problems immediately.

2. The Sense of Powerlessness in Prayer;
   Not Confusion, Nor Malaise

For some, the sense of powerlessness or helplessness in
prayer is mistaken for confusion or malaise. But little
confusion occurs in the prayer of powerlessness since it
reveals starkly that only God can rescue the beloved person or
the situation. And the sense of powerlessness is not malaise, a
debilitating loss of hope and energy for God and others.
Rather, in this prayer the sense of powerlessness discovers

hope and paradoxically restores energetic action. Besides, malaise is often the state of prayerlessness which, far from being prayer, is a total lack of concern for God and his interests.

Instead, prayer of powerlessness is characterized by these six paradoxical notes implicitly revealing strong concern for God and his people.[4] For example, in this prayer one finds a vague feeling that the Lord would like something more, yet this more remains undefined. The praying person asks: "Am I to change to another more fruitful apostolate? Should I be more generous and disciplined in my present work? Is there something additional that I should be doing for my family, my friends, my religious group? Should I be less comfortable? Is there something that stands between me and the Lord?" This questioning is not an ill-at-ease confusion which enervates one's efforts and which paralyzes one's ordinary planning. Instead, paradoxically it tends to make one ready for change should a clear response to these questions arise; it acts rather as a stimulant to reflection than as an oppressive state leading to depression; it leads to closer cooperation with comrades in a more effective apostolate.

A second characteristic of the prayer of powerlessness is that the Scriptures seem, temporarily at least, inapplicable to one's life, while at the same time, paradoxically, they appear to teem with meaning. It is as though the Word of God is so rich that one is overwhelmed and finds one's life quite tawdry in comparison, hardly worthy of scriptural application— except when one contemplates the needs of God's people (Mt 25:31–46).

In a third characteristic, the praying person is aware of a strong desire to let the Lord lead wherever he wishes. Still, paradoxically, the same person is fearful of where the Lord will take him or her. The latter asks deep within the self: "Who am I that God should take me seriously enough to have special plans for me? Do I really want to please him or am I deluding myself here? Do I want to be special in the eyes of the Lord or would I actually prefer to lie hidden and safe within the vast human race?" These are the subtle questions which accompany the strong desire to let the Lord lead wherever he wishes. They make the praying person wonder whether Jeremiah's image of the divine potter molding the clay to his least wishes (Jer 18:3–6) is an inhumane exaggeration; and yet this same person will be simultaneously concerned about personal competence to serve well the particular people whom the Lord has entrusted to him or her.

In a fourth characteristic of the prayer of powerlessness, the praying person, filled with the sense of helplessness before the mystery of life, remains nevertheless competitive, success-seeking, tempted to please others even at the expense of his or her own values, and quite preferential about the persons with whom he or she will work or take leisure. Yet this person is fascinated by death, the ultimate stripping away of friendship, honors, prestige, and sense of accomplishment.

As the praying person looks over the album containing the pictures of friends now dead, he or she notices how many of these people are more simple, honest, generous, and gracious than the one gazing at their pictures. An inner dialogue begins: "Are these thoughts the harbingers of that final stripping which every man or woman dreads? So, where is the sturdy faith in God's providence and in the future life with that great community beyond the grave?" This expresses the fifth paradoxical note of the prayer of powerlessness: an unwillingness to be stripped of power is balanced against recognition of the inevitability of the stripping and against the need for trust in God's providence.

This paradoxical quality of the prayer of powerlessness induces a puzzling ambiguity. Thus patience with ambiguity becomes its sixth characteristic. The praying person asks the self: "Do I fast or pray or do penance to make myself irresistible to God so that I can control him for my purposes? Do I offer myself totally to him in order to win him over to my private providence? What is behind my wish to gain his love more and more through all I do? Indeed, do I use my very sense of helplessness to manipulate him for my own designs? Is my so-called poised freedom (Ignatian indifference) one more ploy in my armory of tricks, the subtlest form of self-centeredness?" Patience with the ambiguity of such questioning enables the praying person to live with the ambiguous events of daily living (e.g., a person's rigorous search for truth ends up in the half-truths of bigotry; the joyous celebration of a marriage anniversary produces promises of divorce proceedings; the thief's attempt to be honest gets him a longer jail term; my apology for a thoughtless act is completed by an unexpected insult).[5]

But neither in life-decisions nor in prayer of powerlessness does one make peace with ambiguity of person or situation as though ambiguity were the deepest explanation of reality. Rather, one uses penetrating intelligence to grasp the murky structure of person or situation and decisive experimentation to outline its limits. Meanwhile, one learns to trust while some of this ambiguity is being dissipated and some of the hitherto hidden mystery is coming to view. Thus the prayer of powerlessness is not a wallowing hole for ambiguity. Instead, it is a living with ambiguity in trust of God and others until, through intelligent inquiry, this ambiguity does partially or wholly disappear so that the underlying goodness of person or situation may appear.

Because of these six characteristics, the sense of powerlessness in prayer is not confusion, nor malaise. Rather, it is a realist view of self and life, together with a profound trust in God as one meets the ambiguities and the paradoxes of one's comrades and one's life-situation. Thus the prayer of powerlessness readies a person for change and for the attempt to find and to do God's preferences—despite fears of what this may mean for one's future. Without disquiet, under the challenge of Scripture and death, it lives with frequent questioning of motives as it keeps the praying person alert to questionable ambitions and unrealistic hopes.

In this way, prayer of powerlessness enables the praying person to live more intimately with the provident God and hence to wait more patiently for the beloved spouse, the close friend and the fellow religious to share their lives more deeply. Thus the resiliency of one's prayer life with God readies the praying person to enter into intimacy with all the dear persons entering his or her life. For the prayer of powerlessness in marriage, friendship and religious vowed life includes all the intimate reality, bad and good, of the people and of their situations. It is fundamentally a surrender to God and to his people in trust.

3. The Powerlessness Found in Gospel Personages

To clarify further what is meant by powerlessness in life and prayer, it might be wise to reflect upon Gospel personages. For example, Mary, the mother of Christ, felt powerlessness intensely once she had spoken her fiat: "Let it be done to me as you say" (Lk 1:38). She gave classical expression to this paradoxical event of powerlessness with her "Magnificat" prayer: "God who is mighty has done great things for me" (Lk 1:49). Then came her inability to tell Joseph of her innocent pregnancy, her difficult trip to Bethlehem at Augustus' whim, the birth in a stable at an innkeeper's suggestion, the flight into Egypt under Herod's threat, the return to Nazareth out of fear of Herod's son, her puzzlement not only at Simeon's prophecies but also at her twelve year old son's reply to her worry ("Did you not know that I had to be in my Father's house?" —(Lk 2:49).[6]

Again and again, she felt her helplessness in the seeming refusal of her Cana request, in the apparent snubbing of her later concern over Jesus' health, and in her heartbreak at the foot of the cross supposedly consoled with the words to her and to John the apostle: "Woman, there is your son; [son,] there is your mother" (Jn 19:26–27). Seemingly at the mercy of people and events, Mary is nevertheless found at the center of the praying Church just before Pentecost (Acts 1:13–14). Her powerlessness is filled with the power of her Son and his Spirit. She knows deep intimacy with both God and her Christian community.[7]

Christ's life is also emptied and made powerless: his birth as a helpless infant, his hurried flight with Mary and Joseph into Egypt, his strict obedience to them in Nazareth, his hidden life there supporting Mary and himself with handyman tasks, his baptism against the Baptist's inclination, his temptations at the repulsive hands of Satan, his endurance of constant personal attacks by the Jewish leaders, his work crippled by the miraculously cured when they broadcast his deeds and thus raise false expectations, his betrayal by Judas and then by Peter despite his warnings. All this culminates at Gethsemane where he accepts the terrible will of the Father in his prayers of powerlessness. His last dark words of total helplessness: "My God, my God, why have you forsaken me" (Mk 15:34)?—in the Greek: "Why have you left me an orphan?"—ironically highlight his final act of trust: "Father, into your hands I commend my spirit" (Lk 23:46). Nothing remains to be given to the Father.

This empty powerlessness is later shown to be full of the Father's power: "Full authority has been given to me both in heaven and on earth; go, therefore, and make disciples of all nations. . . . And know that I am with you always, until the end of the world" (Mt 28:18–20). Jesus promises that his power (found in his own human powerlessness) will be present within our powerlessness whenever we act for him. The suffering servant of Isaiah has become the king of the universe. His very helplessness has rendered him the intimate master of his apostles, his disciples, and the women who followed him from Galilee.

John the Baptist followed closely in the footsteps of his master. Though Christ estimated John to be the greatest prophet born of woman, nevertheless Yahweh allowed John to undergo bleak powerlessness. He sent John into desert isolation while still a young boy having only the skill of survival, then suddenly summoned him out of the desert to baptize under the surveillance of the Jerusalem leaders, later had him give up his best disciples to the Christ, still later let him be hounded, captured and casually beheaded by Herod in the lonely dungeon. Yet has not this noble powerlessness of the Baptist been his Christ-like power over our hearts for twenty centuries?

Again, the apostles, one by one, had chosen to follow Christ in his powerlessness. They had the opportunity to

watch the rich young man refuse to be powerless in poverty
and in loyalty to Christ (Lk 18:18–25); they observed from a
safe distance the Sanhedrin condemn the powerless Christ so
that the politicians could retain their priestly, economic and
political power. The paradoxes of powerlessness became
dramatically present in them, when, during their terrorized
living after the crucifixion, the risen Christ appeared in the
upper room to lend them his own power to forgive sins (Jn
20:21–23), to expel demons and to heal the sick (Mk 16:17–
18).

A last example of scriptural powerlessness is seen in Paul
of Tarsus. The powerful Paul watched and approved the
murder of the helpless Stephen, then received from the high
priest the power to arrest and imprison Damascus Christians
(Acts 9:1–2), but finally was leveled by Christ on the road to
Damascus. Blinded and led by the hand to his Damascus
lodgings, he awaited powerless the healing power of Ananias
to whom Christ had said of Paul: "This man is the instrument
I have chosen to bring my name to the Gentiles and their
kings and to the people of Israel. I myself shall indicate to him
how much he will have to suffer for my name" (Acts 9:15–
16)—how powerless he will feel in prayer and labor while I
work my power through him. This would become the motif of
Paul's life:"I willingly boast of my weaknesses instead, that
the power of Christ may rest upon me. . . . For when I am
powerless, it is then that I am strong" (2 Cor. 12:9–10). Was
this also the source of Paul's intimacy with the risen Christ,
and would this be the source, too, of his compassion for, and
hence intimacy with, all Christian sinners?

Not only are those close to Christ often made powerless
but also Christ describes his kingdom in terms of
powerlessness. For the beatitudes and the woes announced by
Christ (Mt 5:3–12; Lk 6:20–26) are a complete reversal of
the values accorded to secular power. The powerless are the
fortunate ones; the powerful in riches, security, and the good
life are the unlucky people. This is a chosen powerlessness or
at least a faith-filled acceptance of it. It is not the
powerlessness of those who have grasped for economic or

political influence and have fumbled it away. For Mary chose powerlessness with her fiat which, like an explosive, blew up all her plans for the future and left her at the mercy of the Christ events. Christ, too, chose the helplessness of a Nazareth hired day-laborer and of a prophet (whose death warrant was written inevitably by the Jewish tradition). John the Baptist chose (and rechose each lonely bleak day) to be merely a voice crying out in the desert—how powerless can one be?—and to end up a readily expendable pawn for the reckless Herod. If one chooses or accepts such powerlessness, does one also choose or accept intimacy with Christ and with his people?

When one sounds out one's own fears, even strong hatred, of powerlessness, it becomes evident that it is something to be chosen or accepted against all one's natural instincts. Who wants to be stripped of everything—even by Christ? For involved here are *my* talents, opportunities, education, friends, tools of trade. What of *my* plans, liberty, vows and promises? What of recognition in *my* field of endeavor? At stake here is *my* personality development, even *my* weaknesses and limitations, *my* ability to become what others think I should be, *my* career. At all times I must be the professional in control of *my* work, *my* values, *my* destiny; I must have control at all times over *my* feelings, *my* time, *my* self-image. God cannot be allowed to put *me* into the wilderness as he has done with others. For *my* services are too valuable to God and to his people. I do not want, therefore, to be washing the feet of any disciples in a final demonstration of *my* helplessness before *my* enemies. This powerful fear would seem to indicate, then, that scriptural powerlessness is something chosen or accepted only against strong opposite inclinations. Would such fear also explain why we dread the intimacy of scriptural powerlessness as much as we may secretly want it?

Could it be that St. Peter's attractiveness for most people is that he fought off any suggestion of powerlessness until the very end? Peter, the aggressive and take-charge apostle, very likely fumed at his inability to catch fish during various crises,

at Christ's command, "Get behind me, Satan" when Peter
suggested that the powerlessness of the passion was not for
Christ, at James' and John's jockeying for the right and left
seat of power around Christ, at the slowness of the other
apostles to speak out their loyalty during the Last Supper—all
this despite Christ's early warning during Peter's grand
confession of Jesus' messiahship: "Blest are you, Simon, son of
John! No mere man has revealed this to you, but my heavenly
Father" (Mt 16:17).

Peter's powerlessness would, however, become plain to
him at his triple denial of Christ in the courtyard of the high
priest and again at the triple confrontation with the risen
Christ on the shore of Lake Tiberias where his helplessness
was rewarded with the power of primacy in those tender
words: "Feed my lambs, Peter" (Jn 21:15–17). Do we each
see in Peter our struggle against scriptural powerlessness and
our future surrender to it? If this be the case, then how does
this sense of powerlessness express itself as convictions in our
prayer and life? How does this scriptural powerlessness lead
inevitably into intimacy with Christ and with his people inside
marriage, friendship and religious vowed life? These questions
deserve immediate answers.

4. Powerlessness: Its State, Attitudes, Prayer, Mystery

Powerlessness is not simply one item; it is soul-state,
attitudes, prayer, and mystery. It is a state of soul insofar as it
is the discovery that the beatitudes in themselves are
foolishness unless they are announced and warranted by
Christ since he alone is the reward of the beatitudes. He
literally is the reign of God amid our helplessness, the
consolation amid our sorrow, the inheritance amid our
destitution, the fulfilling holiness amid our emptiness, the
mercy amid our vengeance, the single-heartedness amid our
duplicity, the peace-making amid our violence, the serenity
and joy amid our being persecuted. Powerlessness as a state of
soul is, therefore, a "being with Christ's *anawim*, the
dispossessed and marginal people," just as each apostle is

defined as one who has been with Christ (and thus with Christ's people) from the baptism of John until the resurrection (Acts 1:21–22).

Basically, powerlessness is more than lack of control over events. It is choosing to let the *anawim* take over in one's life (for example, their poverty partially dictates the poverty of the one serving them) since they particularly embody Christ. In this way, I let Christ, in his people, possess me more and more. Thus I give up autonomy over my life in the spirit of a Vincent de Paul, a Francis of Assisi, or a Francis Xavier or a Thomas More or an Elizabeth Ann Seton. This tough intimacy or scriptural powerlessness can also be seen as the soul-state in which a person prizes intimacy with the Lord far beyond all his or her busy doings to preserve a successful career, to execute ambitious plans, to attain prestigious position—the attitude of Mary of Bethany at the feet of Christ amid the hurryings of Martha.[8]

Such a state of soul naturally is composed of various attitudes toward powerlessness—for example, the attitude that "one does what one can" amid severe limitations. Such was the attitude of the women going at dawn to the tomb of Christ with the burial ointments. A second attitude might be a willingness to risk coming "just as I am" into the situations to which Christ sends me; there is need for someone to patch up the quarreling factions in a sophisticated parish and I feel somewhat intimidated by my fellow parishioner's better education and expertise, yet I try the patch-up. A third attitude toward powerlessness could be the conviction that, since Christ's powerlessness seems to be his trusting dependence on (his union with) the Father in the midst of dangerous situations, then one's own trusting dependence on (union with) Christ necessarily will include tension, misunderstandings, risks, perils, and the "stretch" (reaching out to do what God wants when I feel not fully equipped to do it). Thus my intimacy with Christ impels me to enter intimately into the lives of his *anawim* as one of them.

These attitudes toward scriptural powerlessness do not rise, of course, without steady prayer of powerlessness. Is this prayer, then, a desire to let Christ work through one's powerlessness (one's inadequacies, sins, limitations, failures, and ignorances accepted trustingly) so that he accomplishes what he wants (not what I want) often without my being aware of his power working through me? If so, then this prayer will often feel ambivalent: yearning to do more, but not knowing what this more is; overwhelmed by scriptural richness, yet finding Scripture inapplicable to daily life; desiring to let the Lord lead while fearing his path; fiercely competitive while pleading one's helplessness; vigorously resisting surrender as one tries to trust God's personal care.

Is not this prayer of powerlessness, then, much more than merely enduring the lack of control over myself and my situation? Is it not, first of all, a great contentment to simply be with Christ and with his people and to let them be free of my ambitions, my manipulation, and my need to control everything? For was this not Christ's prayer when he overcame temporarily the three temptations to exercise raw personality power, political power, and religious power and when he was temporarily left by the Father with no strategy for founding the kingdom? Yet this prayer is no limp passivity. For Christ began his kingdom-work with this prayer of powerlessness so that the Father's power could be exercised through his human powerlessness in doing remarkable deeds for his people.[9]

If these are the soul-state, the attitudes, and the prayer of powerlessness, then its mystery comes to be expressed in paradoxes. Thus, the reward of the prayer of powerlessness is more powerlessness, that is, greater dependence on, and therefore greater intimacy with, the powerless Christ in his powerful Father. Indeed, because prayer of powerlessness contains prudent fear of failure in one's work and prayer, it makes trust in the Father a way of life for the apostle.

Further, God reveals his grandeur to me insofar as I find out my own littleness—my limitations, weaknesses and sins—since the latter are the frame for his power. My powerlessness, therefore, becomes the place where the Father exercises his power most unmistakably. For the apostle's sensitivity to the needs of his people, his ability to console them most effectively, and his awareness of how central Christ is to healing and life may all be products of the sense of his own powerlessness. What else accounts for the remarkable change in Peter and in the other apostles if not the impact of that empty, directionless time from the crucifixion to the Pentecost experience? Here the apostles achieved a depth of intimacy with Christ and the Father, which few of them had envisioned for themselves because of their natural hatred for powerlessness. Here, too, they could discover the intimacy of their mutual companionship in desolating sorrow and fear as well as in consoling hope and joy. Once they had received this double gift of intimacy, they must have found it beyond all price, even the price of life.

Yet even if these paradoxes be true, a problem remains: How is one ever lured to move into this state, these attitudes, this prayer and this mystery of powerlessness? For penetrating vision and much endurance is required to recognize in them the gift of intimacy with God and with his people.

5. Sources of Strength and Vision for Accepting the Intimacy of Powerlessness in Life and Prayer

There can be little doubt that Christian marriage requires the sacrament to make it possible. For the demands of Christian marriage are beyond the human person's natural behavior. In a divorce culture, to pledge lifelong loyalty to the spouse is foolhardy for those under forty. The apostles, well aware of their own divorce culture, were astounded at Jesus' teaching: "Whoever divorces his wife and marries another commits adultery against her; and the woman who divorces her husband and marries another commits adultery" (Mk 10:11–12). So, their cynical response sounds quite just to twentieth century ears: "If that is the case between man and wife, it is better not to marry," to which Jesus would later coolly reply: "Not everyone can accept this teaching, only those to whom it is given to do so" (Mt 19:10–11).

This challenge to the twentieth century couple planning marriage reveals how necessary is the sacrament of marriage for the strength and vision to carry out a pledge of intimacy "till death do us part." Here Christ fills the spouses' empty helplessness with his own presence to all their economic, psychological, and parental problems. In this way he enters intimately into their mutual love as this love struggles with these problems. For this reason, Christian marriage is not merely a metaphorical sign to express how Christ wishes to be united with the spouses. It is much more. Because of its being a sacrament, it contains the very intimacy of Christ simultaneously present in each spouse. As a result, their intimacy with each other compenetrates and blends into each's intimacy with Christ.

Here the covenant of sacramental marriage becomes the covenant of Yahweh with his chosen people. Because sacramental or Christian marriage is this covenant, it must be kept till death since Christ's faithfulness to his people is present in and symbolized by this marital covenant or solemn promise. Thus the sacrament of marriage is both a promise of God's presence to all marital trials or joys and an efficacious cause of faithful intimacy between the spouses and with Christ amid their trials and joys. It does take three to get married as Christians. Human powerlessness, amid the perils of marriage intimacy, needs the strengthening presence of the mediating Christ, the great lover.

Another source of strength for Christian intimacy is friendship. For when friendship is deep, long-lasting, and capable of enduring the separation of distance-time-fights-sufferings, it gradually develops an implicit vow of "forever." Indeed, such friendship acts as a quasi-sacrament since to reduce it back to mere acquaintanceship (the cooled friendship) is to experience vast emptiness, heartbreak, even a loss of faith in friendship, if not in Christ.[10] This demonstrates how Christian friendship, with all its perils, has to contain the reassuring presence of the Spirit of Christ. For Christian friendship is among the strongest bonds uniting Christians in the body of Christ, his Church.

Besides, it is a gift beyond one's expectations and virtues stricken, as they are, with sin and limitations. Perhaps this is why friendship is such a pleasant surprise, is so treasured for its rarity, and turns out to be such a strong bond among God's people. Its intimacy is purchased with not a little sharing of Christ's passion and not a little experience of his resurrection joy. So fragile is this intimacy in its human powerlessness that it dramatizes the strengthening presence of Christ within it.

There is yet a third source for the intimacy of powerlessness in life and prayer: the religious life of the three explicit (public) vows of poverty, celibacy and obedience. These vows act as a quasi-sacrament insofar as they are vows made to God first and principally but also made with and to the community because of its Christ-approved way of life. Since the religious community is a symbol of the future great community of the great tomorrow (the communion of saints), its life-demands are meant to be more than challenging; they are meant to be excruciating as well as beatifying. They are excruciating in that religious poverty is a selfless common sharing of time and things; for it does away with ownership of all the things which promise security. As a result the religious can be insecure in solidarity with the *anawim* who constitute the first members of Christ's kingdom. This is its secret beauty.

Further, celibacy is meant to reduce the urgency of blood ties so that religious are free to move anywhere and to suffer anything in the service of God's people. It is a risky love embracing all the needy no matter what their condition may be. Lastly obedience is meant to assure that the Lord's preferences, rather than career considerations, are followed in the teamwork of meeting the needs of the Lord's *anawim*.

These life-demands of the religious vows are beatifying, too. For poverty does link religious closely in a shared life, celibacy offers a warm brotherhood and sisterhood, obedience provides a deep mutual respect in cooperative apostolate.[11] Such religious life promotes friendships so that a double bonding, natural and vowed, lends strength and wisdom for dangerous risks. For religious are expected to be revolutionaries in speaking out for the poor and in acting freely against the cultural currents which dehumanize and de-Christianize people. In living this way of life, one encounters rich opportunities for intimacy with God, with the brotherhood and sisterhood and with those served by religious because all share the sense of powerlessness.

The stable intimacy so achieved makes religious life an apt symbol for the risen life after death even as dedicated religious paradoxically risk death to make earthly life more human and Christian for others. Certainly, the prayer of powerlessness becomes as necessary for religious as for friends and married people. For their vows strip them of power bases in riches, family, and career. Their only defense is the intimacy of brotherhood and sisterhood with the risen Christ. Personal ties rather than secular powers are the source both of their powerlessness and of their power in Christ.[12]

6. Powerful Conclusions

If the scriptural powerlessness discovered in the perilous living of Christian marriage or friendship or religious life offers paradoxically rich opportunities for intimacy, then it is very important to learn now to live patiently with this powerlessness. This reveals the strategic importance of the sacrament of marriage, the quasi-sacrament of long-term friendship, and the quasi-sacrament of the vowed religious life. But none of these ways of life can be strong without regular prayer of powerlessness. For, even though (unfortunately) this prayer can be mistaken for the state of prayerlessness, still reflection reveals it to be the prayerful way of Christ, Mary, John the Baptist, and the apostles (especially Peter).

In other words, as the prayer of powerlessness strips away our illusions about human autonomy, shows us our basic emptiness, highlights our weaknesses-sins-inadequacies, and renders us compassionate toward, rather than judgmental of, ourselves and others, it paradoxically prepares us for the power of Christ even though we may be quite unaware of this. It makes us persons of the beatitudes, needy, ready to be rescued by Christ, in solidarity with all fellow sinners and believers, eager to help the *anawim* of Christ, and hungry for God's preferences though fearful of them. In such prayer of powerlessness, the Lord can confide his powers to us in Christian marriage, friendship, and religious living.

In startling contrast to this, Ezekiel (34:1–11) speaks of the delinquent shepherds pillaging their flocks and lording it over them because the shepherds (the Israelite leaders) had forgotten their powerlessness and inner trust in Yahweh. They had forgotten that the Lord is dependent on them to shepherd the flock only so long as he wishes to be dependent. They had forgotten that the world of the shepherd is God's world, not the world of the bully and pillager.

Once we the shepherds (parents, friends, religious, professional people, skilled workers, teachers, union organizers, government leaders, entertainers) recall these facts and appreciate our own powerlessness, then we achieve the peace of avoiding excessive concern. We need never again be distraught, only concerned normally, at the scandals in Church and country, at nuclear warfare and violent international blackmail, at third and fourth world injustices, at the lack of leaders in state and Church. To admit simultaneously my own powerlessness and the Lord's intricate and omnipotent providence is to achieve a serene wisdom so that I can work energetically with these problems according to hope and charity, not according to desperation and violence. This is the importance of prayer of powerlessness lived out in daily duties.

Stage Seven
Prayer of Being: Intimacy at
the Self's Quiet Center[1]

Not a few people lose heart when God is drawing them
into *prayer of being,* prayer of simple presence. Here is where
people feel most useless to God and to themselves, most
empty and unworthy of God. For this prayer is quite silent,
ordinarily dry, sometimes hollow, occasionally angry-
fearsome, briefly joyful, and lacking many former certitudes.
If ever a praying person feels far from intimacy with God, it is
at this critical growth-point of developing union with God.
Here, then, such a one needs reassurance against diffidence.
Perhaps assurance will be gained (1) if this *prayer of being* is
recognizably described within one's prayer experience, (2) if
its nature is revealed in Scripture, (3) if the disciplining action
of this prayer can be sketched accurately, and (4) if the way of
living in this prayer can be clearly depicted. All these "ifs"
form the strategy of this Chapter.

1. How to Recognize *Prayer of Being*

Prayer of being, lying hidden underneath at least three
layers of experience, has paradoxical features. Probably this is
because the depth at which *prayer of being* occurs makes it
describable only in limit-statements. The latter plot out the
extreme boundaries of any mysterious experience; they do not
offer a clear x-ray picture of its inner structure.

For example, the first feature of this *prayer of being* is its
wordlessness. When one prays, there seems to be no
response, no sense of God's even hearing one's attempts to
reach him. The silver arrows of one's petitions seem to hit the
tabernacle and to fall shattered at its base. Praying becomes
like the mocking echo of one's own voice when shouting

90

across a river to a great bluff on the other side. At the same time, paradoxically, the prayer may be noisy with distractions. One's mind feels like a huge warehouse at which gigantic "semi's" are unloading fresh cargoes of distractions on the warehouse dock and fork-lift trucks are delivering the boxes of distractions to the center of one's attention.

Naturally, such distractedness is accompanied by extreme dryness, the second characteristic of *prayer of being.* One feels no steady satisfaction, few lifts of the heart with joy. One gains no splendid insights to light up one's path; not even the tired insights of past years arise to illuminate the desert darkness. There is little or no heartfelt attraction for Christ, for Gospel reading, or for generous actions; there is only a certain blankness of mind and a wrinkled leathery feeling in the heart. Yet at the same time, after one has weathered the time given to this prayer (e.g., early in the morning) and has started toward breakfast, one experiences a quiet worthwhileness and even a restored strength for the day's duties. These qualities are palpably missing when one omits this prayer; instead, one knows an indefinable sense of loss and a certain lethargic heaviness.[2]

Of course, such experience seems somewhat hollow, the third feature of the *prayer of being.* The absence of satisfaction felt inside oneself is matched in one's outer activities. Hobbies, entertainment, daily work, favorite diversions—all seem strictly routine, not attractive, and rather superficial as though the silence and dryness of prayer had seeped into one's more exterior doings.[3] Yet in the *prayer of being* itself and in these activities, there is a remote sense of fullness as though through the deepest caverns of one's praying-working self there runs a great underground river. This remote fullness expresses itself indirectly when the praying person finds the self saying: "Where else would I want to be than here? Nowhere else. What else would I rather be doing? Nothing else." What is this peculiar sense of rightness amid silence, dryness, and hollowness? Only later on in this chapter will we surmise its meaning.

Although the person, now doing the *prayer of being,* has already been living faithfully with the Lord not a few years, still a fear may rise that he or she is backsliding, is falling into a web of self-delusion. Yet at the same time this person may feel deep anger toward God at the "unfairness of it all." This is the fourth feature of the *prayer of being.* For the individual begins to question: "What am I doing wrong that the Lord should be so distant?" and then begins some rummaging around in the past for a disastrously wrong decision, a fatal flaw of character, a refused grace of strategic importance.

For example, a retreatant kept asking himself these questions during his Ignatian thirty-day retreat and got this answer on the nineteenth day: "This retreat is a fraud; your life leading up to this retreat has been equally fraudulent; in fact, you've been embezzling yourself from adolescence till now." His director listened to this "dazzling insight" and then said: "Be sure to keep up this type of questioning. And don't for a moment trust yourself, others, me, or God." This response shocked the retreatant into recognizing how superficial was the evidence which provoked the questioning and how strong was the serenity which lay deep in the center of his being—paradox of paradoxes. Even as he felt himself caught in swirls of confusion, he also knew that in the depths of his being he was resting at home with the Lord in the center of the universe. He felt like the weather-pilot who, fighting a bucking plane through the tornado, has suddenly broken into its quiet eye.

But often where there is fear, there is also an accompanying anger. Frustrated with my work, my family, my own self, and embarrassed by my anger at God for all this frustration, I am restlessly eager to break out of this suffocating cocoon of self. Repulsed by my negative mood, by the stark vision of my sins and limitations, and by my own littleness compared to God's greatness, I experience a profound, but false, sense of guilt. For I have forgotten that one gets most deeply angry only with those one loves best and that to be angry with God is to take seriously his goodness and his providence. Anger with a friend (even with God) can be a secret compliment.[4]

Thus the angry Jeremiah felt free to call God to his face "a treacherous brook" (Jer 15:18) and to accuse the Lord of duping him (Jer 20:12). For this reason, guilt at my anger is a false guilt which acts like a suit of armor so that I cannot feel God's touch. Even if I did feel his touch, I would deny it because "why would God want to deal with me?" Yet, eventually, as a fearful, angry person who is doing the *prayer of being,* I find myself repeating the words of the fiercely angry prophet in the Book of Lamentations: "The favors of the Lord are not exhausted, his mercies are not spent. They are renewed each morning, so great is his faithfulness" (3:22–23).

Amid all this confusion, there are occasional leaps of the heart at God's dim presence. They are very brief and widely spaced; yet in a rare moment God may seem to take over completely. Thus *prayer of being* is not one long monotonous bore. A person can, however, overlook these quick touches of the Lord. Once a directee confessed: "If I had not kept a daily diary of this dry prayer of mine, I would have complained that God was completely absent these past fifty days. But when I read back, I found four or five spots where the Lord made his presence felt for a few moments." Of course, this information makes quite a difference not only to the directee but also to the director. So, *prayer of being* is not a state of prayerlessness; its fifth feature is the Lord's quiet signaling of his companionship in our fears and anger.

There is, nevertheless, in this *prayer of being* a gradual loss of youthful certainties. This constitutes its sixth characteristic. One feels quite uncertain about so many things: political issues, the nature of holiness, the future of the United States, theological schools of thought, personality theories, economic cure-alls, long-standing family arguments, the proper raising and education of one's children, and so on. This deep wondering issues not so much from tired cynicism as from a new sense of mystery. Too often the failure of simple solutions has proved the mysterious complexity of a

person or of a situation or of some vast plan of social
improvement. Sometimes the praying person mistakes the
deep wondering at such failures for a faith-loss—especially
when a glance at the vine of one's apostolate seemingly
reveals only shrunken grapes.[5]

A compelling temptation can then arise to find new works
to do, new people to consult, new plans to promote. There
can be even tears at this point though one is not sure why
they come—frustration, hope, self-pity, consolation? The
most acute suffering occurs when the praying person feels
searing doubt about whether he or she can love anyone fully
or be lovable to anyone else. And yet as the praying person
descends down deep into the self without knowing what lies
ahead, there is no desire to go back up even though the
darkness seems to be heavier at the moment. For one
experiences a strange contentment with the situation—
because one feels loved intimately?[6]

2. Does *Prayer of Being* Deny Intimacy?

These six characteristics of *prayer of being;* wordlessness,
dryness, hollowness, fearsome anger, rare inbursts of joy, and
loss of certainties would seem almost to deny the presence of
any intimacy in this prayer. But the opposite is true. First of
all, only by going through the various stages of prayer which
require deep intimacy (one-to-one prayer, forgiveness,
sinfulness, apostolic "more," and powerlessness) can one
enter into the *prayer of being.* To declare that these stages of
intimacy lead only to non-intimacy is to join the absurdist
philosophers in stating that the human person is a living
contradiction built for self-destruction.

In fact, the state of dryness experienced in *prayer of
being* is normal for all prayer just as it is the normal condition
of any human relationship. It is the area lying between the
extremes of consolation and desolation, just as the dryness in
marriage or in work is the normal feeling between the ecstasy
of love or high success and the despair of lost love or
bankrupt business. Dryness in prayer is the balanced state for

enduring well everyday living. It is a secret strengthening joy; it is that sustaining intimacy which arises out of suffering well with the beloved the everyday routines of prayer and life.

Indeed, this dryness is very instructive for the praying person. It forces one to distinguish the various levels of human experience, to enter their depths, to learn more accurately the meaning of passive prayer, and finally to develop a faithfulness to God which is more independent of consolations or desolations, of elations or depressions, and of subjectively estimated successes or failures.

Let us glance at these levels of human experience so as to better understand dryness in prayer. There is, first, a superficial level which presents to our awareness pleasures and pains like the constant purr of an air-conditioner, the heavy perfume of lilacs, the irritation of a skin rash or a raspy voice, the comforting warmth of a May sun or the soft touch of an April breeze and shower. The first level, then, is a constant stream of sensate impressions, the context of life.

Underneath this is a second level of deeper experiences, such as the constant ache of neuralgia or the deep pleasure of loving intercourse or the delight of solving a perplexing business problem or the lyric leap of an evening at the symphony or the exuberant planning for the first baby or the panic fear of a flashing knife. This second level is more meaningful and lends greater depth to the first one.

But underlying both of these is a still more profound set of experiences which make up the third level. It is at this level that one experiences the enervating worry at not having a job, the satisfaction of affectionate family living, the sorrow of watching the alcoholic spouse struggle for respectability, the fulfillment of a successfully completed project demanding ten years of one's life, the sense of worthwhileness in the costly sacrifice for the beloved. At this third level the deepest hopes are raised or dashed, the finest joys are brought into full bloom, and the most crushing sorrows test the stamina of a person's very being.

Believe it or not, there is yet a fourth level, which is the dynamic basis of the three upper levels of experience.

Although the top three levels are directly knowable to oneself, this fourth level is discovered and known only indirectly, that is, only in contrast with the other three. Thus a woman can be in good health on the first level, can be enjoying a full family life on the second level, can see her role in life as richly meaningful on the third level, and yet be restless and pain-filled on the fourth level. If it were not for this dramatic contrast with the top three levels, she could not possibly come to know the fourth level as part of her experience.

This revealing contrast can also occur in the opposite manner. A man may be suffering from a fourteen-day cold on the first level, feeling somewhat misunderstood by the family on the second level, experiencing sharp doubt (on the third level) about his ability to handle the new and complicated position in his corporation, and yet be peaceful at the fourth level underneath the disturbing events of the top three. He could well find himself asking: "What's wrong with me? I should feel depressed and desolate, but I don't. Am I becoming schizoid? Or have I lost interest in my family and my career?" But this startling contrast lets him know, if he reflects on it, that there is a fourth level in his experience, one known only by contrast with the upper three levels.[7]

This long explanation is meant to lead to the conclusion that extreme dryness of prayer at the top three levels of experience can be accompanied by a serene peace and a sense of personal worthwhileness lurking underneath at the fourth level. Such a discovery lights up *prayer of being* since such prayer happens at this fourth level where one comes into contact with one's personal being, one's fullest identity.

Here, too, is the best rendezvous point for meeting God. As prayer of powerlessness has hinted, God is the one doing the praying in us; and he starts it at the fourth level, then lets it percolate up through the three other levels. In *prayer of being*, however, God may shut off this percolation into the top three levels. When this happens, one can find God only indirectly, through the contrast of the upper three levels with the fourth level. At this point the praying person finally recognizes that he or she is totally at the mercy of God's initiative. Again, he or she more sharply appreciates the need to be more passive under God's action.[8]

Most of us, nonetheless, fight hard to be the active senior partner in prayer and so we struggle mightily on the top three levels to keep control. At the first level we may try new vocal prayers, new Zen techniques, new spiritual reading books; at the second level we may try to pump up old emotions once felt and duly inscribed in our spiritual diaries or we may review magnificent panoramic insights of our personal salvation history. On the third level, we may investigate our motivations for being good family people, for becoming career enthusiasts, for entering the life of religious vows, for being unmarried or married, for being lazy or aggressive, for being liberal or conservative, and so on.

In other words, to avoid the passivity of prayer, we strain to climb the sheer glass mountain of mystery by our fingernails. Inevitably we end up at the bottom of the mountain, looking at our bloody hands. Slowly it dawns on us that maybe only God can get us to the top of the glass mountain, that we have to rest passive in his hands as he lifts us gently and gladly, that only after we admit our total dependence on him will he be able to lift us to the top of the mountain. We learn, then, what the passivity of prayer is: letting God do the praying in and through our four levels of experience while we simply furnish ourselves and some basic conditions for prayer, e.g., time carefully set aside, some reading of Scripture and other spiritual works, a reverent body-position, fasting, a readiness to go in prayer wherever the Lord leads, and so on. These conditions God can use or not use as he sees fit.

There is a third result of recognizing this fourth level: because of dryness at the upper three levels, one develops a faithfulness to God which is more independent of consolations or desolations, of elations or depressions. One has finally become aware of the constant presence of God in this fourth level. There, like a great underground river, he quietly nourishes all one's activities on the top three levels. This renders the praying person serene in the sure direction of the river and lets the person know that he or she is never alone, never far from the center of the universe. This quiet reassurance can occur in the midst of the most joyful or the most sorrowful happenings on the upper three levels and thus it nurtures the independence of the praying person. Not surprisingly, it takes the edge off deep fears, dampens down fierce angers, and tends to still pestering doubts. Such experience is hardly hollow in its fullness.

Thus *prayer of being* is never a lonely experience since it is a constant, indirect awareness of God at one's deepest level of awareness, at the center of one's being. In this way, divine being speaks within the individual person's being. Paradoxically, such communion is wordless at this silent depth. It is a simple presence to each other like that between long-married partners who have great mutual devotion to each other. In this one-to-one awareness, God and the praying person have, by a kind of osmosis, an underlying indirect appreciation of each other rather than a direct face-to-face meeting as in the beatific vision. Their co-presence is more by being than by insightful action or by tangible feeling. It is as though the praying person reaches behind his or her back to touch God. For each affects the other by pure presence of being, as happens when people are aware of each other even though physically separated by vast oceans and by towering mountain ranges. Because this presence is so deep and subtle, it takes long years and much experience for the average praying person to recognize its potential for intimacy.

Such mutual awareness is a being-for-the-other. This has a remarkable effect on the human partner. He or she finds greater empathy for other human beings at a deep level of experience, namely, that of being or of radical personhood. It is this which enables the praying person to enter more profoundly into the routinized lives of other sufferers and to feel more deeply the emptiness of their sometimes meaningless lives and the gestureless silence of their listless suffering.[9] As a result the person in *prayer of being* becomes more ready to sacrifice, more apostolic in intent, in order to fulfill the needs of the Lord's *anawim*. Perhaps this is the cosmic compassion of which Christ speaks: "Love your enemies, pray for your persecutors. This will prove that you are sons of your heavenly Father, for his sun rises on the bad and the good, he rains on the just and the unjust. . . . In a word, you must be made perfect as your heavenly Father is perfect" (Mt 5:44–48).

Because this *prayer of being* issues in close union not only with God but also with his marginal people, it leads to a dynamic compenetration of the two great commandments. To love God is to love neighbor and vice versa. In this way, *prayer of being* becomes like the background music permeating my consciousness as I wait for a client to work over financial accounts or have my teeth cleaned or do housework and gardening. It is a quiet, strengthening, enlivening presence which I may even take for granted until its temporary shut-off leaves me cold and bereft. Perhaps better, it is like a long-term friendship highly prized yet often taken for granted because it has always been there to guide, invigorate, and challenge me and, finally, to assure me of a happy future in serving others. Thus *prayer of being*, if it is anything, is a new depth of intimacy not only with God and self but also with all other human beings.

3. *Prayer of Being* in Scripture

Prayer of being is profoundly embedded in Scripture. For, among the multiple tanslations of the divine name Yahweh in the Old Testament, is: he-who-is-for-others. Since Yahweh is the continuing creator and perduring animator of all things, he clearly lives up to his name. He literally brings all things into being out of nothingness and then remains in them to pulse their existence constantly lest they sink back into nothingness. He is being-for-all-other-beings. It is no wonder, then, that in the *prayer of being*, the praying person becomes so sensitive to nothingness or emptiness at the same time as he or she notes the fullness of being around and in him or her.

Yahweh, nonetheless, is not satisfied with this degree of intimacy within all created beings. Out of all the nations, he selects the weakest one, that motley throng of Jacob's descendants mixed with slaves and hangers-on from Egypt, and begins to form them into his people. To do this, he makes a convenant with them; they are to be his people and he will be their God. Actually, it later becomes a marriage covenant since he comes to consider the Hebrew nation his bride. To demonstrate this, he even tells Hosea, who had unfortunately married a woman turned prostitute, to love her yet more. In this way is symbolized Yahweh's marriage with his adulterous Israelite nation. This action dramatizes the intimate relationship which Yahweh wants with the Hebrew people—a relationship far beyond, yet built out of, the intimate relationship of creator and creature in being. Thus any turning of the Hebrew people to a false god is considered nothing less than an adultery to be punished, for example, by the great exile of 587 B.C.

Such a being-for-others (Yahweh himself) makes understandable why the second person of the Trinity would be sent into the womb of Mary to become the Jesus of history. The Christ intimately immerses himself in the being and life of his Jewish family, his town of Nazareth, and his country of Palestine. Jesus becomes Jewish from the soles of his feet to the top of his head. Thus he literally is the wedding covenant of Yahweh with the Hebrew people; his very flesh and all his historical actions are divine and human, Godly and Jewish, inextricably.

In this way, the God-man can enter into and share our gestureless-wordless silence in the hidden life of Nazareth, our routinized dryness in his daily handyman tasks, our felt hollowness in his self-emptying sacrifices for us (Phil 5:2–7), our fears ("My soul is troubled now, yet what should I say— Father, save me from this hour?"—Jn 12:27) and our angry frustrations ("What an unbelieving and perverse lot you are! How long must I remain with you? How long can I endure you?"—(Lk 9:41). He also can share our rare leaps of joy ("At that moment Jesus rejoiced in the Holy Spirit"—Lk

9:21), and our dwindling certainties (the three temptations or strategies for the kingdom which were rejected by the Father without any further direction) and the consequent tensions felt at the center of our beings (Jesus stretched out with the sleep of exhaustion in the storm-tossed boat). He knew all the ingredients of being human; he, too, did the *prayer of being* to the Father. Within his bones and nervous system Jesus felt his being-for-others operating at the three upper levels of his experience.

This being-for-others is best seen, however, in his joy at the fourth level which underlay his passion on the upper three levels. The seven last words of Christ express an exquisitely beautiful and expensive intimacy. When Jesus said: "Daughters of Jerusalem, do not weep for me. Weep for yourselves and for your children" (Lk 23:28), could he have been other than a being-for-others amid terrible dryness and felt fear? When he cried out: "Father, forgive them; they do not know what they are doing" (Lk 23:34), was he not a being-for-others amid the deaf silence of his crucifiers? When he turned his head toward Dismas to say: "This day you will be with me in paradise" (Lk 23:43), was he not a being-for-others in the brief joy of this moment? When he looked to Mary and John and said: "Woman, there is your son; [son,] there is your mother" (Jn 19:26–27), was he not a being-for-others emptying himself of his last possession? When he screamed out: "I am thirsty" (Jn 19:28), was he not revealing that his being-for-others felt hollow and dry in its helplessness? When he spoke to the Father appealingly: "My God, my God, why have you forsaken me?" (Mk 15:34) was he not a being-for-others feeling the loss of cherished certainties? When in a final burst of profound trust he shouted: "Father, into your hands I commend my spirit" (Lk 23:46), was he not a being-for-others stripped down to nothing but trust, having given over to the Father all that was dear to him: Mary, the apostles, Mary Magdalene and the other loyal women, his work of the past thirty-five or so years, and the whole future of his Church?

Underneath this crush of events commemorated by Jesus'
seven last words, underneath the excruciating agony on the
physical, psychological, and spiritual levels of Christ's
experience, is the fourth level of his joyous strength in the
Father's love for him and in the beautiful background music
of the Father's tender, caring affection for him. For the death
of Christ on the three top levels was simultaneous with the
subdued resurrection on the fourth level. Would this not be
Christ's continual *prayer of being* within the paschal mystery?
Has there ever been such intimacy in suffering and joy as that
of Christ with the Father and with his people? Thus is
revealed dimly the structure of the *prayer of being* beneath its
previous paradoxical features. As the author of the Letter to
the Hebrews notes: "For the sake of the joy which lay before
him he endured the cross, heedless of its shame" (12:2).

4. The Terrible Liberating Discipline of the *Prayer of Being*

The *prayer of being*, therefore, carries within it a terrible,
yet beautiful, discipline: the willingness to suffer for what is
right and just, true and good. The author of the Letter to the
Hebrews puts the meaning of discipline bluntly for us:
"Endure your trials as the discipline of God who deals with
you as sons. For what son is there whom his father does not
discipline? If you do not know the discipline of sons, you are
not sons but bastards" (12:7–8). Evidently God disciplines his
people out of affection by allowing them to suffer.[10] As a
result, aware of their powerlessness, they can be endowed
with his power without any fear that they would claim this
power to be their own.

Chapters six to nine of Deuteronomy illustrate how a
terrible discipline prepares for intimacy with God, for the
prayer of being. There God declares: "You shall not put the
Lord to the test" (6:16), that is, demand that he act in your
way at your time and place. Clearly, "It was not because you
are the largest of all nations that the Lord set his heart on you
and chose you, for you are really the smallest of all nations. It
was because the Lord loved you" (7:7–8); in your littleness

you do not set the music of the dance with God. "For forty years now the Lord, your God, has directed all your journeying in the desert, so as to test you by affliction and find out whether or not it was your intention to keep his commandments . . . the Lord, your God, disciplines you even as a man disciplines his son . . . [lest] you become haughty of heart and unmindful of the Lord" (8:2, 5, 14).

God's guidance through the desert (of *prayer of being*) may seem directionless to us and may seem to undermine our certainties. But our trustful following keeps us from the crazy deviations of pride and of secret contempt for God's providence. This discipline of the *prayer of being* is necessary because: "Otherwise you might say to yourselves, 'It is my own power and the strength of my own hand that has obtained for me this wealth.' . . . No, it is not because of your merits or the integrity of your heart" (8:17; 9:5). This last statement is strangely reassuring for the person doing *prayer of being* and feeling virtueless, angry, fearful and empty. Such a person has reason to hope because Christ anticipated all this: "Son, though he was, he learned obedience from what he suffered; and when perfected, he became the source of eternal salvation for all who obey him" (Heb 5:8–9). There is, therefore, a scriptural basis for the discipline found in *prayer of being*.

The discipline itself, though painful, is actually a liberation produced by the *prayer of being*. Such liberation, however, is not a secret contempt for the bodily and the sensual; this would be a disincarnation, not an incarnation, of Christ. Nor is this liberation the ability to leave a beloved person or a favorite place-possession-job-ambition without suffering regret; this would be more a cold self-centeredness which is ready to detach itself only in order to grab something or someone else better. Rather, this liberation is:

(1) a willingness to be separated from what one loves for the sake of the beloved without ever ceasing to love this beloved (seeing off the missionary friend without hope of ever meeting again);

(2) a willingness to let someone dear grow freely, without trying to control, even though this means great suffering for both (the parent letting the stubborn twenty year old son make a drastic mistake in choosing a job—for the sake of his growth in wisdom);

(3) a willingness to risk everything to put God or another person ahead of one's business, sporting success, work, comfort, or career, even as one continues to pursue these ventures;

(4) a willingness to choose the good consistently, in a disciplined way, despite the pain involved (the isolation of the scholar pursuing alone his quest for truth);

(5) a burning hunger for God's preferences, no matter what the price, simply because one trusts the Lord's affection and his wanting only the best for oneself (as does the man who is wheelchaired into the emergency room during a heart attack with his wife and two oldest children tagging behind);

(6) a trustful submission in one's *prayer of being:*

   (a) to God's silence (as his quiet word nevertheless sounds his desires in one's heart);

   (b) to God's dryness (as he lets one's life-routines seem so little rewarding);

   (c) to God's darkness (as the superabundance of faith-light awakens one to overly ambitious plans and to overlooked limitations, sins, and inadequacies);

   (d) to God's aloof majesty (as when, in one's fear and anger, he appears to be unaware of one's child undergoing shock treatments for depression and later refusing all attention);

   (e) to God's seeming neglect of oneself (as he gives only rare pats on the head);

   (f) to God's seemingly directionless guidance in one's life (as one finds certainties diminished: one's loyal friends, the teaching Church, job security, family, economic future).

And all this liberation (this gradual detaching from what one too much clings to) is allowed in order that God may empower one in his own way, own time, and own place for hopes which God alone presently knows. Clearly, *prayer of being* is expensive in its suffering of God's discipline. It is, nonetheless, at the same time a quiet yet deeply joyous intimacy with God and his people at the fourth level of one's experience.

5. The *Prayer of Being* in Daily Events

If this prayer is so demanding, one may ask: How does one live with it—even though one may agree that living without it is intolerable? It would seem to put the praying person between the classical Scylla and Charybdis; you suffer if you do not live *prayer of being* and you suffer more if you do live it. For *prayer of being* is more an attitude toward God, self and others than any particular action. So, the first way to live this *prayer of being* is to trustfully submit to the God who prays this prayer within oneself. No other decision is quite so intimate, quite so demanding. This is evident from the sixth feature of *prayer of being:* God's discipline mentioned immediately above.

A second way to live this prayer is through "the prayer of centering." I sink deeply into myself to find God at the center of my being and I discover that God is more intimate to me than I am to my own self—a fact noted by Augustine in his fourth century *Confessions.* This prayer of centering enables me to find my lasting home, to uncover the fact that the center of the universe is within me. This changes my perspective on all the events thrusting themselves upon me. People become much more important to me than success and things. Life is stripped down to essentials. Respect for myself grows. Silence no longer stifles me. Hopefulness in others takes deeper root even when their style of life differs markedly from mine. God's providence is seen in smaller details of life so that I feel tenderly cared for. In other words,

I become more trustingly submissive to God—not with the passivity of the bathroom rug, but rather with the passive alertness of the good listener who is ready to respond sympathetically when the listening is finished. Yet, as always, there are times of fear, anger, confusion, worry, amid occasional eruptions of God's felt presence.[11]

In *prayer of being*, I am tempted to let God be God. This means that I do not try to imprison God inside my present conception or image of him. I may even let God break my idol-images of him, no matter how elaborate the conception, no matter how comfortable I am with a particular image and how uncomfortable with some new image crafted by traumatic events. Every person knows that God is greater than any idea which he or she may have of him, but to admit that God is quite different from what one had first thought is both startling and fearsome. For any new image of God requires a new relationship with God and sometimes a large change in one's life style.[12] This alert passivity is a third way of "doing" the *prayer of being*.[13]

Thus this prayer humbles a person before God as Moses found himself prostrate before the burning bush or as Peter fell on his knees before Christ at the miraculous catch of fish: "Leave me, Lord. I am a sinful man" (Lk 5:8). The overwhelming greatness of God literally grounds me in my own smallness and I nod assent to the harsh words of Christ: "When you have done all you have been commanded to do, say, 'We are useless servants'" (Lk 17:10). This stark realism of the *prayer of being* leads the praying person to appreciate the wry wisdom of St. Vincent De Paul when he said to the novice about to work with the destitute of the Paris slums: "If you really love the poor, they may not resent your charity so much." Hence with the *prayer of being*, there is a humility which readily sees humor in overly solemn people and occasions. Is this humor itself an expression of *prayer of being?*

Such humor is needed because *prayer of being* puts one into contact with the priesthood of the faithful, a life of sacrifice (and secret joy) for the people of God. This is the life of the paschal mystery specially symbolized and carried in the ordination of deacon, priest, and bishop but also shared in one's baptism-confirmation by every lay person serving Christ's people. The *prayer of being* alerts the praying person to the fact that every action performed for others is also the act of Jesus Christ, the high priest, energizing the actor within his or her very being. As a result no action is without deep meaning because each has eternal effects; "As often as you did it for one of my least brothers, you did it for me" (Mt 25:40). Every service of the Christian is Christian because it orginates with the priestly Christ present in the person serving, and then returns to the same Christ dwelling in the person served.

Thus the Father (by sending Christ to be our high priest) and his Son Jesus (by exercising his priesthood within us) initiate the *prayer of being* which is to direct our service of fellow Christians. Next, this service, itself filled with the *prayer of being*, enters into the life of the Christians who are being served. In this way it enters the body of Christ where Christ can return such service to the Father. Thus is completed the grand circulation of divine life. Is our alertness to this circling of grace a fifth way of living the *prayer of being?*

For this reason, no sacrifice for others, no apparent lessening of one's own being to enhance the being of others, is ever lost. Each sacrificial act finds its way to the Father through the Son, where it lives on forever, never to be underestimated, never to be forgotten, never to be lost. This is what *prayer of being* reveals to us since it is centered within our own immortal being and since it meets there the eternal being of Christ and of his Father. As a result, there is a sustaining joy underneath all the sacrifices of the priesthood of the faithful. This is a joy so deep within the Christian that he or she would not appreciate it unless the *prayer of being* were operative. It is, therefore, a quiet joy. Actually, it is a rocklike confidence in God, self, and others; it is a homing toward the Trinity.

Now since *prayer of being* is a total and constant movement of one's being and not merely this or that dramatic action, it is very quiet in us and hard to discern without guidance from another. Because it is a continuous and never-ending life, there are few abrupt contrasts of presence and absence, few quick changes in quality, to reveal its presence energizing every action one performs. Thus the *prayer of being* puts one into intimate contact with one's own basic identity as well as announces the active co-presence of God. Of course, such prayer requires times of deep recollection and is discovered ordinarily within great suffering.

For this latter reason, one lives the *prayer of being* by asking for the gift of the third mode of humility described so acutely and briefly by Ignatius Loyola in his *Spiritual Exercises:* "Whenever the praise and glory of the Divine Majesty would be equally served, in order to imitate and be in reality more like Christ Our Lord, I desire and choose poverty with Christ poor, rather than riches; insults with Christ loaded with them, rather than honors; I desire to be accounted as worthless and a fool for Christ, rather than to be esteemed as wise and prudent in this world. So Christ was treated before me."[14] The attitude behind the choice of such a life is a pure gift from Christ; it is not some noble decision that a person makes. For this gift contains the being-for-others prayer at white-hot intensity; it is the baptism of fire for which Christ was in anguish till he received it (Lk 12:49–50). This gift is at once the fiercest and the tenderest intimacy, for it contains the most intense faith-presence of Christ not only in the serving person but in the *anawim* who are being served.[15]

Further, it involves a preference for seeking out the marginal, broken, contemned people simply for the reason that they are foremost Christ's people. Only a fierce love for Christ could get the serving person to enter the marginal people's lives, and only a fierce love of God could get the marginal people to accept the humiliation of being served at the center of their beings where they are most vulnerable to the manipulators. This is the intimacy of the *prayer of being* and, perhaps, the deepest way of living it.

Indeed, it is an intimacy which not only describes but accomplishes God's act of identifying with (marrying) his universe and his people. Consequently, this intimacy is a secret strength, a perduring hidden joy, felt precisely at the same time when suffering and sorrow are stabbing at the heart. Not surprisingly, then, the author of the Letter to the Hebrews reiterates that Christ's sufferings under obedience brought his love to fullness (2:17–18; 4:15; 5:8–10; 9:14); and at the same time John the Evangelist's whole Last Supper tract is a remarkable affirmation of the quiet profound joy underneath Christ's sufferings and sorrows (esp. Jn 16:7–21).

Here, too, within this *prayer of being*, lies the peace with which one discerns whether or not a decision is a following of the Lord's preferences. It does not give certitude, as though it were a spiritual litmus test for validity. Rather, it simply assures one that he or she sincerely wants God's will, and is ready to suffer a lot to accomplish it. After all, since we are fragile, fumbling creatures, the best we can do is to try to accomplish God's preferences. This is why those earnestly endeavoring to do God's will may undergo not a little darkness and suffering, silence and emptiness, waiting and chafing. But they are doing the most God can ask of them; they are *trying* to accomplish his will. If *prayer of being* leads us into this attitude, it is well worth the price it costs.

6. A Harrowing Conclusion

At last we know why we sometimes say to the person offering intimacy (and especially to God): "Go away closer." Intimacy is literally a suffering and a joying at the center of one's own being, where one is most vulnerable, and at the center of the other person's being, where the other can be destroyed most easily. Both the risk to the self and the obligation toward the other can be fearsome. It is, therefore, a harrowing time of silence, concern, emptiness, fear of self-delusion, lessening of certainties, and anger of frustration—along with tantalizing touches from God. It is the call to become a being-for-others like God himself, Yahweh. It is a

call to the discipline of deep, lasting friendship, to the
liberation from pettiness and from mere self-interest, to
trustful submission to the other, to the allowing of others to
grow beyond one's solicitude for them, to the risk of entering
the priesthood of the faithful and of asking for the gift of the
third mode of humility. Yes, intimacy is what we most want in
all of life and also what we most fear—and justly so.
Surprisingly, *prayer of being* is the deepest, most quiet, most
lasting joy underneath all life's rigors and vigors.

Stage Eight
Trinitarian Prayer of Intimacy: Ultimate Communion of Persons, Divine and Human[1]

Finally we reach the utlimate lure drawing us all into intimacy: a compenetrating union of persons in their bodies, minds, hearts, spirits, lives and hopes—the fullest and deepest community. This is the radical source of all embracive feelings, knowings, lovings, persons, families, and even nations. This is what the human heart unrelentingly longs for. But why would a good God ever let this desire arise in us, if, seemingly so often, it is to remain empty and thus mock us? Could it be that God is not capricious but that some basic fear in us thwarts us—and God?

Here we enter into the area of the prayer of ultimate communion—a communion for which, again, every person yearns and so few seem ready. Do we not all fear the prayer of ultimate communion? Is this because we all dread the possible loss of our identity, of our personal consciousness, in some all-absorbing power? At this point does not the thought of God's vast majesty overwhelm us? Perhaps if we can bring ourselves to explore what the ultimate communion of intimacy is and how it is attained, we can be less fearful of and more open to our future with God and with others. Then, if this happens, the prayer of ultimate communion may seem much less fearsome to us and the above questions may find some answers.

1. What Is Ultimate Communion, Radical Intimacy?

What is this ultimate communion, this future great community, which is the source and goal of all intimacy and which may perhaps be operating within the prayer of ultimate communion? If one were to describe ultimate communion as the compenetration of persons, what would this mean? Such compenetration is beautifully symbolized, at the physical level of life, by marital embrace and intercourse. The latter requires that the partners be stripped of everything except their selves, that each concentrate on the other's pleasure and joy, that each reassure the other's confidence, that each trustingly gamble his or her very being on the other's faithful response, and that both continue to show affection long after the completion of the peak-act of intercourse.

Here the physical union symbolizes a more important underlying element of marital love: the psychological compenetration of minds and hearts over many years. In this affective union, the lovers learn to reverence each other's personality (that integrated totality of all one's knowledges, values, skills, imaginative sets, virtues, routines, hopes, idiosyncrasies) in all its bodily manifestations: the wide smile, the quick shrug, the tears, the grace or awkwardness of movement, the angry glance, the erratic car-driving, the fearful shudder, the brisk or langorous walk, the flow or hesitancy of speech, the unique flair of dress. Marital intimacy moves toward a total embracing of the other person in all the latter's many personal aspects, both the good admired and the bad not admired.

This psychological unity which underlies the couple's physical reactions reveals, in turn, the spiritual blending of man and woman in marriage. This spiritual compenetration is the sharing of their deepest mutual values, hopes, fears, experiences and loves. Without this spiritual blending, the psychological unity eventually begins to deteriorate into spiteful spats and coolness, while the physical unity of embrace and intercourse becomes a mockery for both partners—a ritual without meaning because spiritless and irreverent.[2]

But when the partners' hopes and experiences more deeply compenetrate each other's spirit, then each partner's value so grows in the other's eyes that they would gladly die for each other. For nothing else, except God, rivals this ultimate value of their spiritual intimacy. Then, if they ultimately believe in God's presence within each other and within their future together with God, the resurrection is already taking place within them. For the incipient resurrection is their continually growing love for each other and their increasing mutual union with the risen Lord.

Thus their resurrection goes beyond their union of bodies and of spirits to include the compenetration of their very beings in an immortal embrace of the now eternal Christ. The frustration of intercourse where they must part, time after time, to lead somewhat separate lives is far less. And the frustration of "temporary divorces" during temper-tantrums and mutual cold-freezes diminishes. Now their lives are woven tightly because their very beings now compenetrate in a never-to-be-ended union. Further, within this mutual compenetration of their beings is God pulsing their beings with his being. In this way, they are truly married to God within their own married bodies, spirits, and actions. There is a type of trinity here of the couple and of God in a union which is meant never to end. This is the couple's temporal stability, their strong hope for the future, their eternal living (now happening in time).

Nor does this quasi-trinitarian union absorb the couple in such a way that they lose their identity to God, no more than their marriage has meant that one spouse has absorbed the other. Quite the opposite. The developing union of husband and wife has been contributing to the uniqueness of each because each has been adding strength, knowledge, ambitious energy, and values to the other for the latter's unique integration of these gifts. In a similar way, the indwelling God's gifts of enthusiasm, inventiveness, wisdom and hope to each of the spouses make each more, not less, unique. Thus, as each grows in this way, each has more to offer both to the partner and to God and each enriches the other commensurately.

This indicates that their married love can continue to grow after death and that the compenetration of their very beings becomes richer and more intense as the years and eons

pass. With this added richness, each can better appreciate
God. In thus valuing him more, each becomes more closely
united to him. As a result, he can further enrich them both
with all his wealth of being. Such a benevolent circle of
growth can begin to accelerate in this dynamic trinitarian
relation between the spouses and God. Indeed, unlike the
interstellar rocket, the acceleration need never stop. Is it this
ongoing life of the married with God which is to be feared? It
would seem not.

But, then, could the fear be of suffering? No doubt this
ultimate communion, though it ends up in heaven,
nevertheless starts here in this life before death and is
presently well disguised by its tensions and ordinariness. For
marital love has to perdure through foolish arguments,
grocery-buying routines, breakfast silences, threatening
home-mortgages, vacations more expensive than anticipated,
sick children, jobs lost and gained, births and deaths,
graduations and grandchildren. Because of all this, humor, fun
and play are essential to such communion. For these
spontaneities teach us loving patience with each other as they
arise out of a compassionate sense for the high ideals of
married love and the sometimes ludicrously lower living of
these ideals. Do we fear the embarrassment and suffering of
patience? This would not seem to be the case for most people.

One sees this exasperating and yet humorous contrast as
Christ washes the feet of his apostles. There are dropped
towels, spilt water, Peter's puzzled protests, Christ's
challenging responses to Peter's remarks, the awkwardness of
the apostles at being treated like nobles by their admired
leader. He wants so much to show them how he affectionately
reverences them, and they do not know how to act. Yet at the
same time something exalted and serene is happening as one
reads on in John the evangelist's account of the Last Supper.
Underneath all the awkwardness of washing the feet of the
apostles, Christ is expressing a faithful and familiar affection
for the apostles. This affection they will never forget as,
through all the ensuing years of tensions before their deaths,

its memory stirs and strengthens them. Such affection, clothed in the bumblings and fumblings of life, is meant to last forever. Is this part of the fear of ultimate communion—a great awe at the nearness of the omnipotent God's affection? Is this why we say to God (as well as to others): "Go away closer"? Is this the source of our fear?

Day-to-day marital living parallels this experience of Christ and his apostles. It, too, is filled with gropings, miscues, awkward gestures, ill-timed ventures; yet all of these are strung along a unifying thread of deep affection. And this love, too, is meant to last forever. Once the married couple becomes fully aware of this thread, they experience quiet exaltation and achieve a serenity which enables them to live together through shattering events and wild arguments. This is the beginning awareness of the ultimate communion between themselves and with God. For the latter is at the center of their beings, encouraging them to love each other forever no matter what happens, giving them confidence that each would die for the other if this were necessary, assuring them of the strength necessary to reach out—sometimes far beyond their expectations—to take within their marital embrace not a few others. In this way they can form the extended family of God around themselves.[3]

Because this embrace includes God, it starts the ultimate communion which will be consummated more fully in heaven. Of course, such an exalted state hidden within the ordinariness of life before death is a mystery to us—a mystery equally present and equally formidable for friends and for vowed religious. Is it any wonder, then, that the prayer of ultimate communion which promotes this compenetration of persons would be something we fear as much as we yearn for it? If we should now consider the supreme example of compenetrative union, that of Father, Son and Spirit, would this allay some of our fears of ultimate union (that radical intimacy of married couples, friends, or vowed religious with themselves and with God) and set burning the desire for it?

2. The Ultimate Intimacy of the Trinitarian Persons

So rich is the divine act of existence that three distinct persons can share it, whereas the lesser human act of existence can support only one person. Because the three persons share the same one act of existence, they totally compenetrate each other; the generosity of each holds nothing back. Yet at the same time, each can distinctively focus the one divine intelligence to understand the other two fully and each can distinctively bring the one divine will to love each of the others completely. Each person, then, has a distinct identity (a personhood) not to be confused with the identities of the other two, and each, therefore, can give the self to the others. So successful is this self-giving that each person totally compenetrates the other two in the one divine act of existence and does this with supreme satisfaction. Yet each person retains personal identity so that the self-gift can be intended forever.[4]

To enjoy such supreme compenetration of being is the destiny for which each human being is made. Each of us, having been created by the Trinity as their image, naturally yearns for such a compenetrative unity and wants to express it from the very springs of our being. Thus, in the Genesis narrative, God brings man and woman together so that they can express their yearning for compenetration of being in their bodies, their minds and their hearts. This union no other human may ever break, since it mirrors the eternal compenetration of the Trinity and later will image the faithful love of Christ for his Church, his mystical body. The marital union of Adam and Eve, then, is meant to be a continual giving of each one's inner wealth of being to the other. If, in this giving, each grows ever more unique and ever more lovable, then at the same time this union between them will grow ever more compenetrating, ever more satisfying.

What is said here for marriage is also true for friendship. If the long-lasting friendship implies a "forever" vow of faithfulness and so becomes a quasi-sacrament in dignity, then its aim is for the friends to mutually enrich each other's being with commonly shared experiences, with common pursuit of truth, and with mutual reverence for each other's person and future. In this way, the beings of friends gradually compenetrate so that the rupture of this friendship would be a tragic divorce at the level of their very beings. For this reason, friendship offers the unmarried and those in a failed marriage a further opportunity to experience and to express that compenetration of personal beings which lies far beyond the merely physical. Thus the faithfulness of friends, over many years and through numerous hardships and joys, enables them to appreciate and to image the Trinitarian compenetration of persons so that their lives are ultimately meaningful and successful.[5]

These ultimately Trinitarian values of marriage and friendship are found at least as richly in the lives of those who have vowed themselves to God and to each other in poverty, celibacy, and obedience. Their common ideals offer a fund of shared values for establishing a life of unity: high esteem for prayer, a centering of daily life around Christ, and the strong hope of life after death. Meanwhile their vow of poverty keeps them from being separated by mounting piles of possessions and encourages them to live a life of trusting dependence on each other. Obedience links them in common work for the Church where cooperation and shared risks foster friendships begun because of interdependent living. In celibacy, they discover the importance of friendship. For they find that the warm bonding which supports them in brotherhood and sisterhood especially unites them with God. The sisterhood and brotherhood are, in other words, based primarily on union with the God to whom they are first vowed and through whom they become bonded to each other in community—the reverse order of marriage. In turn, such friendships vitalize their apostolic work and transform poverty into a concelebration of their life with God's poor.

This basic sharing of values (common life of poverty, cooperative obedience in the apostolate, and celibate brotherhood-sisterhood) assures a gradual blending of these vowed persons in their very beings. This, of course, occurs

within the primary compenetration of being with the God to
whom these religious have first and principally vowed
themselves. Such vowed life is consciously aimed to cause
eternal compenetration of mind, heart, feelings, purpose and
life with God precisely in the brotherhood or sisterhood.
Here, clearly, the ultimate communion of compenetrating
intimacy begins before death and is meant to be completed
after death. Thus, in the lives of vowed religious, one learns
that the prayer of ultimate communion is needed not merely
for pursuing the vowed religious life; it also structures all
Christian life on earth as well as carries it beyond death to life
everlasting in the communion of saints.

It could be said, then, that marriage, friendship and the
vowed life of religious are meant by God to image and (what
is more remarkable) to actually promote the ultimate
communion of compenetrative intimacy. On this account, the
prayer of ultimate communion (or intimacy) looms up in our
consciousness as literally "the be-all and end-all" of life.

Clearly, such prayer and such union can be enjoyed by
non-Christian believers. But they can be more fully lived by
Christians because the latter have explicit revealed knowledge
and sacramentally assured appreciation for their
compenetrative union with the Trinity. For in John's Last
Supper account we discover how much God wants to live his
compenetrating life with each Christian person and
community. "I will ask the Father and he will give you
another Paraclete—to be with you always: the Spirit of truth,
whom the world cannot accept, since it neither sees him nor
recognizes him; but you can recognize him because he
remains with you and will be within you" (14:16–17). Indeed,
"On that day you will know that I am in my Father, and you
in me, and I in you. . . . Anyone who loves me will be true to
my word, and my Father will love him; we will come to him
and make our dwelling place with him" (14:20, 23). It could
not be clearer that God wants and intends to bring the
Trinity's compenetrating union into the compenetrating union
between Christians.[6]

But it is one thing to describe the union, quite another to bring it about. How does the Christian cooperate with God in bringing this union into full bonding? What are, then, the sources of that ultimate communion which is radical intimacy?

3. The Sources of Radical Intimacy

No human would dare to claim for himself or herself the radical intimacy of ultimate communion: the compenetration of persons in their very being. It would appear to be too arrogant if not too risky. The revelations of Christ, however, have depicted this state to be the meaning and destiny of our lives. This revelation begins in the prologue to John's Gospel. Here one finds that the dynamic pattern for all creation is the second person of the Trinity, the Word. The Father, out of love for his Son, created the world according to that wisdom which is the very nature of his Son. As a result, creation not only carries the natural imprint of the divine artisan but also, to the eyes of faith, reveals the inner life of the Trinity. For the universe has the Son's very wisdom for its dynamic plan of existence.

But this divine creative act is not a static moment at the beginning of time; rather, it is an ongoing act moving through all time. In other words, as the world evolves through its unique cumulative growth, it is gradually revealing more and more of the ongoing inner life of the Son. For the eyes of faith, the universe is literally imaging and thus living out the Son's nature, his inmost meaning. This revelation, as we have already seen, is a most intimate act wherein year by year, epoch by epoch, the various aspects of God's inner life become incarnate, as it were, in the evolution of the world and (at the advent of man) in the cumulative development of human history. God, by pulsing the very being of the universe and by inwardly luring man to his destiny, is intimately living in the world and in man.

This first step into radical intimacy leads to a second step, namely, the prophetic revelation wherein Yahweh makes a marriage covenant with his special bride, the Israelite people.

Each of the parties to this marriage, amid their familial squabbles, get to know each other better so that the Hebrew nation truly becomes the bride of Yahweh. This covenant is renewed and deepened immeasurably by a third step into radical intimacy: now the Father sends his Son, the Word, to become unfleshed in the womb of Mary, that is, to enter a human soul and to form a human body. This marriage of the second divine person of the Trinity with a human body-soul to form Jesus produces two results. First, Jesus becomes the flesh and blood revelation of his Father so that every action which this Christ performs is a direct revelation of the Father. "Philip . . . whoever has seen me has seen the Father" (Jn 14:9). Second, when Christ's divine act of existence is united with his human body and soul, he becomes the living covenant of God with the human race. He is the marriage of God and humankind.[7]

This third step of radical intimacy leads into the fourth step whereby Christ bequeathes sacraments to the apostolic Church. For these sacraments are signs of Christ's ongoing presence in the world after his ascension to the Father and they are designed to happen at each critical juncture of a Christian's life from birth to death. They are, indeed, a continuing dramatic proof of Christ's affection and careful work for his people. For, in each instance, the sacraments mark the entrance of Christ into deeper intimacy with the Christian and they assert Christ's continuous presence within each happening outside and inside the individual Christian's body and spirit.

Not satisfied with this, the Father and Christ have sent the Holy Spirit into each Christian to form all Christians into the one body of Christ, the Church. Thus the Holy Spirit becomes the very union between individual Christians and at the same time their divine union with the Father through Christ. For the Holy Spirit is always in compenetrating union with the Father and with the Son who is Christ. This is the final Trinitarian source for that radical intimacy which constitutes the Christian as Christian and which becomes his or her final destiny.

To understand how this giving of the Holy Spirit forms the Church into one flock under one shepherd, one must notice how the sacraments act as signs of this intimate union. For example, baptism signifies the fact that the Trinity is now dwelling in the baptized person as Christ had promised at the Last Supper. It also establishes the fact that now this person is a son or daughter of the Father, a brother or sister of Christ, and a friend of the Spirit-Advocate. Then confirmation reiterates and strengthens this membership in the family of God by adding power to the commission that each Christian bring Christ's message to all the world. Because of this commission, the Holy Spirit forms more and more people into the body of Christ.

Both sacraments alert Christians to the additional fact that they are sharing in the priesthood of Christ whose life of sacrifice intimately strengthens them so that they can intimately strengthen their fellow humans. Meanwhile, the Spirit of Jesus, the advocate or befriender, illumines and directs us in this heroic life of sacrifice which is animating the body of Christ. In the sacrament of reconciliation or penance, the same Holy Spirit reunites sinners with the Church of fellow sinners and thus deepens their intimacy with the compenetrative Trinity and with their fellow Christians. Once again, in the sacraments of matrimony and ordination, the Holy Spirit works to build the body of Christ by fostering increased family and ecclesial life through the intimacy of marital, friendly, and religious love. Lastly, the sacrament of the sick brings the suffering Christian into close rapport with the healing Christ and readies him or her for possible entrance into the ultimate intimacy with the Trinity.

4. The Eucharist, Central Source of Intimacy

It is especially in the Eucharist, however, that one sees the Holy Spirit working to increase the intimacy of all Christians with each other and with God. For the Eucharist is offering intense intimacy with Christ as his body and spirit compenetrate the receiving Christian's body and spirit. Then,

too, the Eucharist acts as the center to which all the other
sacraments point because it is the basic goal from which all
other sacraments derive their meaning. Here the Holy Spirit,
in the consecration prayer of the Eucharistic celebration,
assures us that Christ is entering into the bread and wine to
be received by us as our spiritual food and hence to be
melted, as it were, into our very being. In this way, the Spirit
is presiding over the entrance of each Christian into deeper
intimacy with Christ and, through Christ, into intimacy with
the Father.[8]

Consequently, the Eucharist becomes the foretaste of life
after death where the Trinity's compenetration of our beings
becomes immediately evident to us in what is called a face-to-
face seeing and embracing of God. In this way, the Holy Spirit
produces the compenetration of all lives in Christ now and
after death. Not only does the individual Christian
compenetrate with Christ but all Christians compenetrate
with each other since each and all together enter intimately
into the one life of Christ.[9] Through Christ, each and all enter
into the single being of the Father and the Spirit. But this
becomes palpable and much more fully achieved (rather than
seen only darkly and felt only indirectly through faith) when,
after death, all Christians are united to each other and to
Christ in a single great compenetration of all beings. Then
truly "God is all in all" and we experience the communion of
saints.

The growth of this radical intimacy with the Trinity is not
simply dramatized but is even produced, step by step, in the
Eucharistic sacrifice which both images and causes the union
between Christians and with Christ. Each step leads to a
deeper intimacy between all participants. The first step is
merely the decision of geographically scattered individuals to
gather for the Eucharist out of hunger for intimacy. This
corresponds to that hunger for intimacy mentioned earlier as
Stage One of all prayer. The second step is simply the actual
gathering of God's people to celebrate the Eucharist as they
greet and chat with each other face-to-face. In this it is similar
to the prayer of one-to-one intimacy described in Stage Two.

For the gathering is a necessary condition for the Eucharist to happen just as the prayer of one-to-one intimacy makes possible all other types of prayer. The third step is the admission and confession of one's sins so that one is ready for the shared intimacy with fellow sinners and with Christ who forgives all sins. This is comparable to Stage Three of the prayer of intimacy, that of reconciliation or forgiveness. For in both cases the humiliation of confession fosters a realistic openness to others.

The fourth step toward greater intimacy during the Eucharist is the common petitionary prayer of the congregation as the people admit their total dependence on God for the gift of the world and for all spiritual gifts by which this world is to be enhanced. Here one finds a similarity to the prayer of sinfulness which lets God know that the praying person is well aware that his or her sins and limitations require the inner presence of God if anything good is to be achieved. This, of course, parallels Stage Four of prayer of intimacy. In a fifth step of the Eucharistic service, the Word is first read and then expanded in the homily to give us a wider vision and larger heart for the world and for God. As a result, the hearer can allow God into the self for its conversion. Thus a very intimate moment is reached which is much like the daring prayer of the apostolic "more" of Stage Five. For now the hearer, by the very listening, is readying the self for the entrance of God's expansive presence into his or her life so that he or she can better and more boldly serve fellow Christians—even at great risk.

Later, in a sixth step toward greater intimacy, the gift-offering of bread and wine signals to Christ how powerless the Christian feels to transform himself or herself and the world unless Christ enters these gifts to fill them with divine content. So, they lift to God the gifts which he had previously given them so that he can enrich them more. This reminds one of the prayer of powerlessness of Stage Six wherein one waits confidently and helplessly for the Lord to act within one's skills, knowledges, and hopes. Then, in the seventh step toward radical intimacy, the Holy Spirit acts to make Christ present in the bread and wine—an act celebrated throughout the eucharistic prayer. Here mysteriously the being of Christ replaces the substance of bread and wine so that Christ is totally present, divinely and humanly, in flesh and spirit. As forecast in Stage Seven, the "I AM" of John's Gospel has entered the being of our world to pulse it.

Because of this, in the eighth step where Christ is received within the Christian's very being, the prayer of ultimate communion and intimacy achieves its aim: compenetration of persons. When Christ's being compenetrates that of the individual communicant, his simultaneous compenetration of all other communicants provides a social compenetration of all communicants in their beings.[10] Within this Stage Eight of prayer of intimacy is contained, of course, the firm promise that after death all communicants will know directly (and not merely through faith) that they are compenetrating Christ's being and all other human beings as Christ leads his whole body, the Church triumphant, into fuller life with the Trinity.

The Eucharistic sacrifice, then, recapitulates all the types of intimacy-prayer described in the eight stages. It indicates how they are steps or stages leading ever more deeply into the present and future life with Father, Son, and Spirit. For this reason, we might well explore what this prayer of ultimate communion or intimacy could be in our daily living. Indeed, this present outline of the sources for this type of prayer has shown that the prayer of ultimate communion issues out of the revelatory events of the Old and New Testaments, out of the seven sacraments, and finally out of the Eucharistic sacrifice which acts as the center of all revelation and of all the sacraments. But what does this mean for hour-to-hour living amid work, family, life, leisure pursuits, worries and joys?

5. The Prayer of Ultimate Intimacy in Daily Living

Let us start bluntly and quickly with a definition of the prayer of ultimate intimacy or communion. In this way, we know precisely what we are looking for and we can challenge its truth with our various experiences of prayer. Let us say provisionally that the prayer of ultimate communion or intimacy with God is a profound contemplation-in-action wherein the passive-contemplative is more evident than the active-apostolic although the active becomes more powerful precisely because of the dominance of the passive.[11] This prayer is a daily living of the patristic contemplation-to-attain-divine-love as developed and popularized by Ignatius Loyola.[12]

The first note of this lived prayer is the overwhelming discovery of how central is the divine Word to all history. For the Word is seen first as the dynamic pattern for the evolving universe, secondly as prophetic revelation working within the Hebrew community to enliven the old covenant marriage with Yahweh, next as the incarnate revelation of the Father (the enfleshed Christ of the New Testament), later as the heart of those seven intense intimacies called the sacraments, and finally as the body of the Church formed by the Spirit of Jesus.

This Christ-centeredness, therefore, fills all nature, all technological accomplishments, all developing civilizations, and all cultural achievements.[13] It fills them with inventive verve, with personal concern, with hope in the future, with patience during slow experimentation, and with reverence toward each being. In other words, Christ's central presence as the Word turns the world into a home rather than a place of exile or a hostile prison. The universe is seen as Christ's world and no one else's ("Take courage! I have overcome the world"—Jn 16:33; "Full authority has been given to me both in heaven and on earth; go, therefore, and make disciples of all the nations"—Mt 28:18–19). Thus for a person praying with this ultimate stage of intimacy, the world can become as personal as his or her own life and home.

As a result, the second note of this prayer is a desire to serve the world well, that is, to make it more wholesome with justice, to render it more beautiful with the artistic, to bring it to friendliness with peace efforts, to help it come alive with appreciation of its historical past, its present scientific advances and its spiritual destiny, and to provoke it to deeper awareness of the Christ present in every event. Here we co-create with the Father in Christ. For this service is not that of a subordinate; it is that of a friend with Christ ("I no longer speak of you as slaves, for a slave does not know what his master is about. Instead, I call you friends, since I have made known to you all that I heard from my Father"—Jn 15:15). To be friends of Christ (factually sisters and brothers through baptism) is to feel the reality of the family of God. This is to know by faith that in our beings is the one compenetrating being of Christ.

Consequently, this friendship, the third note of ultimate prayer of union, convinces us that human joys and sufferings are suffused with the provident presence of Christ. This is the communion of ultimate or radical intimacy. John's Gospel makes this fact unmistakable: "I am the vine, you are the branches. He who lives in me and I in him will produce abundantly, for apart from me you can do nothing" (Jn 15:5). But this communion is not only in joy ("All this I tell you that my joy may be yours and your joy may be complete"—Jn 15:11; see 17:13) but also in sorrow ("A time will come when anyone who puts you to death will claim to be serving God"—Jn 16:2).

For John, neither sorrow (the pruning of the vine) nor joy (the bearing of fruit) exists without the other since we each and all are one with Christ in being, life and mission. Thus at times the joy is unbelievably intense; at other times the sorrow and suffering are terribly painful. But in any case, one is never without the other; the passion-death is never without the resurrection moment during our life before death. Again, the prayer of ultimate intimacy or communion is the prayer characteristic of one who is receiving the gift of St. Ignatius' third mode of humility, that is, the gift of fullest life within the paschal mystery—the fourth note of this prayer.

Clearly it is this oneness in suffering and joy with Christ which leads to final intimacy with Christ and, through him, with the Father and the Spirit. Henri Nouwen has suggested that all the physical suffering and mental sorrow of history find their ultimate meaning in the fact that they are revealing gradually, in an infinite number of ways and of persons, how great and varied were the sufferings of Jesus which released us from sin into liberty, from misery into ecstasy.[14] Would this not be true, too, of all the joys and delights in human history? Would they not also reveal, in an infinite number of ways and persons, how deep is Christ's joy in the world and in us? Would this be the innermost meaning of all lyric literature?

Our oneness with Christ, then, is realized in our companionate suffering and joy with him. How deeply one's mind, heart, and body share his suffering and joy measures the friendship one experiences with him—a union paradoxically beyond all friendship. For such union with Christ, then, lifts us, like the apostles, into union with the Father and the Spirit: "I have given them the glory you gave me that they may be one, as we are one—I living in them, you living in me—that their unity may be complete. So shall the world know that you sent me, and that you loved them as you loved me" (Jn 17:22–23). Even the ecstatic Greek philosopher, Plotinus, who is accused of pantheism, had never conceived of a union such as this where the Christian's intimacy with the triune God would be comparable to the unity of the three divine persons with each other. Such intimacy is surely the ultimate communion even if it grows forever.[15]

It is necessary, however, to recall that all the suffering and every sorrow so endured are meant to lead to a greater capacity for joy and to a fuller life of joy not only after death but also before death: "I give you my word, there is no one who has given up home, brothers or sisters, mother or father, children or property, for me and for the Gospel who will not receive in this present age a hundred times as many homes, brothers and sisters, mothers, children and property—and persecution besides—and in the age to come, everlasting life" (Mk 10:29–30). Our God is a God of joy if one judges simply from the feasts of joy inaugurated by Yahweh through the Old Testament narrative.[16]

Indeed, he gave us a sabbath or a Sunday to make sure that we had time for leisurely joy with our family, friends and himself. Clearly, he has made us for joy, unlimited joy; he has not created us for sorrow even though he has let sorrow be the path toward a joy greater than would be possible without sorrow and suffering. Ultimate joy in the ultimate intimacy of Trinity life is what God has been waiting to give us now partially, later fully, and always greater. This fact the prayer of ultimate intimacy slowly reveals to us as we live through the years and the eons.

Up to this point, our focus has been on the action of this ultimate contemplation-in-action (also called prayer of ultimate intimacy or communion). It is now time to describe the contemplative or more passive aspect which has been already broadly hinted in the description of the active element. The contemplation of this prayer, its passive moment, is not merely one's own felt joy in all Christ-centered creation and in all persons crossed by Christ; it is also experiencing Christ's own joy in the world and in his people. This is a double joy. In it one finds Christ taking joy within his brother's and sister's joys and enhancing their joys with his joy—as would be natural for a brother to do. This doubled joy, people report, can become so intense that they have trouble breathing. Here the Father lets the praying person know that he or she is deeply cherished and here the Spirit is recognized as being the very joy experienced.

This immersion in the life of the Trinity, the fifth note of the prayer of ultimate communion, is an awareness of how ultimate intimacy occurs when each divine person gives the self totally to each of the other two persons. In this way, the praying person has a hint of (and a hunger for) what it means to lose oneself in the other and yet to be more conscious of the self than ever before because of the glad reception of oneself by the other. This immersion in Trinity life also alerts the praying person to the way in which each divine person finds happiness in the happiness of the other. It is the Father's delight in his Son and in the Son's Spirit; it is the Son's admiration of the Father and of the Father's Spirit; it is the

Spirit's joy in being the very union, the very intimacy, between the Father and the Son. Thus the praying person finds the self more able than ever to rejoice fully in the happiness of others. There is, again, a hunger to let others be, to let them expand to the limits of their being in all their loves and joys.

Finally, the praying person experiences how each Trinitarian person prays with the total divine self, the sixth note of the prayer of ultimate communion or intimacy. It is an expansive prayer, not merely the emotional and imaginative, not merely body and soul, not merely for this person or event. Rather, this prayer involves the totality of the person stretching to encompass the totality of beings. The praying person understands and tries to love all persons and things in loving each person of the Trinity.

This is the Ignatian contemplation-to-attain-divine-love as it totally occupies the mind, the heart and the body because it issues from the contemplator's very being insofar as the latter is permeated with the three Trinitarian persons. Here the passivity of this ultimate contemplation-in-action can be recognized for what it is: the individual human person being passively compenetrated by the Trinity's being and hence actively compenetrating all other beings of the universe, human and infrahuman.

6. Startling Conclusion?

In the prayer of ultimate communion or intimacy, then, the praying person meets the three distinct divine persons in the oneness of their being, in the closest intimacy possible. Yet each has a distinct identity; each is a distinct person. The Father is found knitting each of us in our mother's womb out of the millions of dancing cells, then molding us by events and by the people of our family, neighborhood, school, work-group, leisure life, religious community, city, nation, finally luring us through all this to the present moment on our way to ultimate community, friendship, and intimacy.

Out of the sufferings of the world (we think of Cambodia, Lebanon, Vietnam, Iran-Iraq, Northern Ireland, Central America, South Africa, those behind the Bamboo and Iron Curtains), the Holy Spirit, our befriender, is lifting good out of evil to build the body of Christ with intimate friendships and with incipient acquaintanceships on the model of the praying person's life of suffering and joyous friendships. Meanwhile, Christ, the Lord of history and the Omega Point to which all converge, is taking into his human personality all that is true, good, and beautiful in all cultures and civilizations. This he does in order to recapitulate them and then to present them to his Father—and (wonder of wonders) to the praying person in his or her day-to-day prayer forever.[17] In this shared work of Father, Son and Spirit is their common love for each other and for each of us. The creation canticle which follows says all this succinctly:

A Creation Canticle[18]

Before the story of your love is told,
We, your sons and daughters (every hair,
Every hair of our heads numbered) shall hold,
Possess in all its essence, fondly praise
Each quick perfection, each particular
Lavished by Love's largess on eye or ear—
Each aurora, skylark, diatom and star,
The interfolded wings of each white rose,
Each blizzard crystal's Byzantine design,
Each cricket's litany, each sparrow's fall,
The rainbow sheen, the shine, the finery
Of every fin and mineral and wing,
The lights, the moods of skylines, mountains, oceans,
And marvels the lightning mind alone illumines—
Philosophies, numbers, norms, inventions, notions,
Each coda, each conundrum, each conceit,
Every right and every wrong,
The lilt, the beat, the brio, the sweet choice
Of syllable and sound in every song

Shaped by every bell-curved lip
In all the dulcet dialects of earth,
And mysteries the heart alone can plumb—
The Eden wonder of each kiss, each birth,
The relentless drumroll coming of each death,
Each laugh, each cry, each clinging last goodbye,
Every betrayal, every loss, every individual cross
We shall own and know and feel and know why
Even as you who know
The curvature, biography, and mass
Of each bubble in the surf, each blink of dew
Diamonding woven web or morning grass,
Who have the measure of each mite of sand
In all Arabia's deserts and mold each face
And fondly trace its changing lineaments
Out of the depth and height and breadth of Grace
That must create, embrace, and sing,
Perfect and love
Every
Thing.

Joseph Awad

Overview
The Ever-Deepening Mystery
of Prayerful Intimacy[1]

Intimacy in itself is a natural mystery of infinite dimensions. That is why we fear it as much as we hunger for it; that is why we act so bizarrely as we simultaneously avoid and pursue it. The phrase: "Go away closer" expresses this attraction-repulsion of every love. But even more mysterious is the prayer of intimacy because it involves more than human love. It also includes divine love. Thus there is the double jeopardy and double allurement of two interlocking mysteries. Has the previous discussion somewhat clarified these two mysteries? If so, the work done is not wasted.

Has this discussion also rendered these mysteries more mysterious? If so, then our entrance into these twin mysteries has been successful. For it is only in beginning to penetrate these mysteries knowingly that one discovers how great and how baffling, beyond any expectations, are their many facets. Could we review, then, the eight stages of intimacy and the eight corresponding types of prayer of intimacy to see whether these eight facets may reflect on each other and so reveal a bit more of these two intermingled mysteries?

1. First Stage: Prayerful Recognition of the Costly Conditions for Intimacy

Admittedly one fears the first intimacy beyond any other experience because it exceeds all previous experience in intensity, tends to put one out of control with joy, and simultaneously demands a fearsome total self-gift. Yet one desires it beyond all else because it claims to give great happiness and, in the lives of some people, seems to fulfill its claim. There is, however, no little ambiguity about intimacy.

It simultaneously encourages and discourages us when we meet the "instant intimacy" of a fellow traveler on a coast-to-coast airflight or the dramatically promising intimacy of a Bahamas vacation for two or the surprisingly easy intimacy with someone (who turns out to be merely curious about one's life) or the strangely absent intimacy where one would expect it in the large family or in the long-term business association or in someone already gifted with many friends or in the novitiate of a religious order.

Because of the wariness learned from this ambiguity of intimacy, we tend to look behind the external expressions of intimacy: the warm glance, the secret language, the smiles, the hugs, the longing sighs, the air of expectancy, the conspiratorial wink, and the gentle touch. But what are we looking for behind these gestures? What is the center, "the more interior intimacy" out of which these exterior intimacies flash? In other words, what are the interior conditions which make intimacy happen between two people? We recall past experiences and slowly build a profile of the intimacy-encouraging person. He or she must have the ability to listen, must be unshockable, should be alert to the needs of others, would likely resonate to the confider's feelings, has to be trusting and trustworthy (will not blab secrets nor give trust too readily), should know how to share mutual hopes and values, and finally must be willing to offer prudent advice and yet be patient when one dallies over decisions or fails in carrying them out. Are we actually describing the Christ-figure here? He alone, it would seem, could adequately fit the profile of these qualities. Have not these reflections already led us unwittingly into the first stage of prayer of intimacy: our very hunger for intimacy?

For this reason, we next probe for what underlies these skills, gifts and virtues of the ideal confidant. What power controls their use? What precisely is this more interior intimacy so feared and so prized, so much a part of one's life yet so rare, so demanding of humaneness? The answer to this question is particularly crucial when one is dealing with prayer of intimacy. For the double mystery of the divine and the human intersect to form a double intimacy within this prayer. In fact, this intimacy runs through the heart of any type of prayer: day-to-day faithfulness, forgiveness, admitted sinfulness, the "more" in apostolic prayer-work, powerless living (in marriage, friendship, vowed religious life), simple being, and ultimate communion.

Each of these types of prayer seems to move gradually into a deeper stage of intimacy with Christ, self and others as each type descends more deeply into Trinity-life by way of intimate sacrament events and by way of scriptural praying and living. If intimacy itself is a mystery, what must prayer of intimacy be? At this stage one has learned to value intimacy above all else—at least theoretically. One is already praying because one already values and hopes to live out the demanding conditions for intimacy with God, self, and others. This praying person now refuses to put God up on a shelf safely above daily life or to treat him like a mere abstract idea. One is implicitly praying with intimacy.

2. Second Stage: The Prayer of Day-to-Day Intimacy

Intimacy is inescapably present in the heart of all life-experience. For we are created with the intimate act of intercourse and with the equally intimate process of gestation in the womb where the mother and child change each other by symbiosis. Creation does not end at the child's birth but continues outside the womb. The child is intimately webbed within the family by language learning, by prolonged education of twelve to twenty years, by child and adolescent friendships, by the emotional stirrings of movies and music, by sorrows and defeats commiserated and by successes and joys celebrated. Intimacy, then, is the implicit source of one's womanhood or manhood; yet, oddly enough, it must be laboriously raised to full consciousness if it is to reach maturity and to render us completely human.

Working within this human intimacy to render it richly conscious, is the Christ of the Gospels who may be met in classroom studies, in the liturgy of the sacraments, in the domestic prayer life of the family and the congregation, in the service of one's fellow human, and particularly in the traumatic events of daily life like birth, death, failure, success, aloneness and worry over one's future. Christ, therefore, can appear within one's life as a constant companion, one in whom a person can confide and expect some response, one who can appreciate humor and meet the surprising event with a smile—even in the most solemn circumstances. He is the one who will lead us to our destined life after death where our happiness will become secure in the intimacy of family, friends, neighbors, and God. Here human intimacy is made vibrant with the life of Christ and of his family, the people of God.

But how does the praying person attain such a living presence of the risen Christ within the self? One watches the Gospel events and tries to imitate Jesus learning, just as we, to become intimate with the Father through day-to-day prayer of intimacy. In other words, Jesus presents himself to the Father face-to-face, alone, every day, growing accustomed to the Father by saturation of experience. This prayer has to be strictly honest, to be ready for increasing trust-demands, to be generous in bearing more and more responsibilities, and to be willing to accept more suffering for others. This is not merely "professional prayer"—rigid, dutiful, carefully controlled, analytic-conceptual, safe. Jesus' prayer to the Father is daring, spontaneously obedient, warm-hearted, reverent, and capable of anger. So much is contained in this so-called "simple," day-to-day prayer of intimacy because it is the root of all other types of prayer, individual or communal.

It is crucial, then, that the praying person follow Christ's path of intimacy with the Father. This means that he or she must be baptized into the inner family life of the Trinity and thus into the daily familial life of the Church. How else be intimate with Christ the second person of the Trinity and the head of the mystical body, the Church? Next the praying person lets the Gospel mysteries, the dynamic memories of the risen Christ living in the baptized person, arise in and gradually possess his or her consciousness.

This is done precisely in the daily prayer of intimacy
where one honestly questions God about one's self and one's
doings—especially when one feels grieved or neglected by
God. There the praying person will experience the creative
aloneness (not the self-centered lonesomeness) of day-to-day,
face-to-face prayer with him. There, too, he or she patiently
awaits some growth of intimacy with Christ and with his
people. For this dogged persistence will be richly rewarded in
the deeper stages of intimacy with others and God—
rewarded surprisingly in manner and in quality amid the
seeming alienation of loneliness.

3. Third Stage: Prayer of Forgiveness

Usually only those intimate to us can hurt us deeply,
unforgettably. Thus their forgiveness requires an
excruciatingly intimate meeting of minds and hearts. Basic to
growth in intimacy is the courage and compassion necessary
not only to forgive those dearest to us but also to accept their
forgiveness of us. Here the radical self-knowledge of oneself
as loving and lovable is attained in the midst of one's painfully
evident limitations and sins. The first time the alcoholic
parent seeks and receives forgiveness from the adolescent
daughter can be the occasion for renewed affection between
them; the event can also contain a heart-searing recognition of
one's lifelong weaknesses. Reconciliation is a costly intimacy
which becomes more possible because of the day-to-day
companioning of Christ in prayer of intimacy.

Nevertheless, we are sometimes counseled: to forgive is
to forget. This advice is deadly. To forget one's hurts and
limitations is to suppress them and to let them thereby
become poisonous so that one turns into a passive-aggressive
toward life. Rather, to forgive is to remember the hurt
without vengeance but with reaffirmation of the offender's
worth. This alone renders forgiveness noble—and very
painful. Then the later restoral of the offender to one's circle
of acquaintances or friends (which may also be part of the
forgiveness) makes the pain even more intense.

All this ordinarily takes time because deep hurt heals only slowly. Indeed, the hurt may even grow after the forgiveness as one better understands the extent of the insult and feels it physically, psychologically, and spiritually. The man who discovers that his business partner and friend has been embezzling their co-owned company over ten years may forgive the offender before it fully dawns on him how much the company's growth has been stunted, how many associates' careers have been damaged, how often during the ten years the offender has expressed apparent friendship, how much the forgiving man's family has lost—at least financially, if not psychologically ("Whom can I trust now?") and spiritually ("Will my children now receive a lesser education?"). As a result, the tough-tender prayer of forgiveness must be happening before, during, and long after the act of forgiveness occurs. On the other hand, for the offender the occasion of being forgiven is an humilating event perhaps long overdue yet nevertheless scorching and hardly forgettable. He rightfully feels, much like the forgiver, that his life is in shreds.

In such circumstances, it becomes painfully clear how necessary is the sacrament of reconciliation for full forgiveness. Where else can the forgiver and the forgiven meet—unless with Christ who is the living covenant of their friendship and who alone can restore the fuller trust required to heal the friendship. But even before this moment (now prolonged through life) there must be in each a scriptural awareness of Christ's own daily tender-tough forgiveness of Pharisees and sinners. Nor will this scriptural awareness arise if it is not provoked by long-term prayer of forgiveness before, during, and long after the act of forgiveness.

Paradoxically one must forgive the other in order to be able to forgive oneself and one's God. For every forgiver has also, along life's way, been the one forgiven. Long after the alcoholic father has been forgiven by his daughter, he continues to recriminate himself, finding it almost impossible to regain his self-dignity. Once, however, he has come to forgive a sister who has maligned him to the family, he may

come to forgive himself for the crime against his daughter—
but only then. And in forgiving himself, he may rediscover his
power to "forgive" God for letting him wreck his own life.

At this point he may even feel the forgiveness of Christ
within himself in his own bitter-sweet tears. His prayer of
forgiveness has reached its goal: a new intimacy with Christ,
with his family, and with himself. Now the sacrament, his
ongoing prayer of forgiveness, and his scriptural awareness of
the forgiving Christ can challenge him to daily, gradually
growing, demanding intimacy with Christ and with his people.
Now the Our Father takes on fearsome depths of meaning
never before suspected. He has discovered that failure to
forgive spreads his venom to ever wider circles of friends and
acquaintances. To forgive, however, is to extend the warmth
of God's embrace to a larger and larger family of God. Indeed,
if I forgive the one who has refused my forgiveness, I may let
Christ do all the healing in both offender and offended and to
free both from their guilts, narrow viewpoints, and
constricting limitations.

4. Fourth Stage: The Prayer of Admitted Sinfulness

The experience of forgiveness sharpens awareness of
one's sinfulness: one's potential for committing any sin
imaginable out of one's drive for identity, sex, career, God
and sheer survival. This sinfulness could easily destroy self
and others by promoting actual sin-acts and by hardening
sinful attitudes developed out of repeated evil choices. For if
sin is what ruptures intimacy, then sinful attitudes crush out
intimacy at every level of life: the physical, the vegetal, the
animal, and the human. Any betrayal of another person
demonstrates that sin is the rupture of intimacy (mutual deep
living in each other's life). By sin a creative union is damaged
and rendered paralyzed for a time since basic respect for life
is dying. And so, everybody loses since no sin is ever private,
ever contained merely within the sinner. In this way, natural
resources are wasted; the symbiotic union with plants and

empathy with animals are ruptured; human relationships become dwarfed and retarded.

In this context, scriptural revelation can be seen as God's great act of intimacy, a supreme self-disclosing, done in order to repair this massive rupture of intimacy. Thus Genesis narrates how sin is a tragic loss of intimacy between Adam and Eve, between them and the now hostile animals as well as the now resistant earth. Consequently, the sharp rupture between humans and God is rightfully terrifying to them. But Yahweh patiently attempts to heal this huge rupture with the Abraham-Moses convenant of friendship, with the strong yet gentle messages of the prophets, with Christ's coming as the living marriage-covenant for the Hebrew people, with the Spirit-Befriender's forming of the people into the one body of Christ, with the intimate sacrament-events meant to heal, invigorate, and direct God's people through all the peak-and valley-moments of their lives.

Yet it is especially the sacrament of reconciliation which encourages the sinner to live beyond the disastrous past, within the cramping limitations, and with honest refusal to be crippled by guilt—because he or she is trusted and loved. At the same time the sacrament of the sick gives insight into lasting values and strengthens us to live them with restored vitality for the sake of the crucified Christ and his people.

Unfortunately, the prayer of sinfulness (which contains all these attempts of God to repair our ruptured intimacies with others and himself) is sometimes mistaken for the state of prayerlessness since both include a sense of loss. The state of prayerlessness is characterized by chronic restlessness-loneliness-alienation, by a continuing estimate that the holy is unreal, by compromising hypocrisy, by chronic manipulation of others and resultant joylessness and finally by a type of passive satisfaction with this state. Thus, for the prayerless person, Christ is no more real than a huge figure on a painted billboard, larger than life but lifeless. Christ counts for little in any important decision of the prayerless person.

Prayer of sinfulness, however, does not have these chronic characteristics though at times there will be in it some experience of loneliness, restlessness, manipulation, hypocrisy, and consequent sense of loss. Therefore it can be mistaken for the state of prayerlessness and, for this reason, the praying person can be sometimes haunted by fear of being in a prayerless state. But, generally, in the prayer of sinfulness there is a sturdy hope in God's generous forgiveness; also a deep joy in his reassuring presence throughout all the praying person's experiences of past sins, personal defects, limitations, fears, and frustrations. One is finally somewhat at peace to live within these restrictions to growth. For this prayer of sinfulness, by making us aware and accepting of all these losses, unexpectedly sharpens our appreciation for our individual talents, hopes, and opportunities.

Thus prayer of sinfulness is ironically filled with gratefulness for God's attentions and with confident energy for spreading his kingdom. So, it turns out to be the safest of all types of prayer because its grounding in reality (its humility) renders us grateful enough to attempt great deeds for God and intimate enough to self, others, and God to escape divisive self-righteousness and to gladly join Christ's Church of sinners. Finally, it enables us to let God run his world in his way with his timing—no small accomplishment in us. Such trust, the fruit of daily prayer of intimacy and of forgiveness, animates the prayer of admitted sinfulness.

5. Fifth Stage: The Prayer of the Daring Apostolic "More"

Valid self-esteem, sensitivity to one's own limitations, and felt gratitude toward God and his people—all generated by the prayer of sinfulness—give the praying person confidence to become an apostle for Christ. As Van Breemen has noted: "True mission comes from remission of sins." Of course, the prayer of sinfulness salts one's apostolic confidence with that genial cynicism which G.K. Chesterton considered typical of the balanced Christian. Otherwise the apostle, in a fit of enthusiasm, might burn out from imprudently igniting all reserve energy.

The prudent apostle, however, working to fulfill the pressing needs of family, city, and Church, is quite aware of the pain coming from accepting and then living prudently within personal limitations. Consequently, this praying person is not without a sense of helplessness due to the enormity of the work compared with his or her own small skills. But the apostle has come to recognize that paradoxically the Lord uses this situation of helplessness to dramatize his strengthening presence within one's work, to sensitize the praying person to other people's sufferings from shortcomings, to strip the apostle down to the simple desire to do the Lord's will and to teach him or her how to pray and work with the liberating conviction: "I am not God but merely his servant." These four qualities are directly the opposite of those found in that burn-out victim called the super-apostle.

Meanwhile the praying apostle discovers the "more," a deep satisfaction, which is the hidden strength and wisdom of Christ within the self. This interior "more" is recognized by way of a second exterior "more," the better-than-usual results of one's apostolic work. For, as the apostle stretches (gambles daringly yet prudently) toward the "more," Christ works through him or her to be "more" present to this praying person and to produce through him or her better results, the "more" of apostolic work. It is here that one experiences the Ignatian "first mode of humility," the willingness to risk anything rather than to fail seriously the affectionate Christ and his vulnerable people.

Now this remarkable experience of the "more" in one's work and prayer is strengthened by the sacraments of baptism and confirmation where one gains the first confidence to commit oneself to service of God's family. Such dedication becomes an intimate cooperation with the people of God and with the Spirit of the Church because of the double sense of the "more." At the same time, the sacrament of the sick may be restoring the health of the apostle physically, psychologically and spiritually. As a result, the latter has "more" appreciation for health, friends, work, skills, and community and learns to let God do some of the worrying. The sacramental joy of life is thus enhanced.

Strength also is coming directly from the apostle's daring prayer of the "more." For in it one discovers, enjoys, and thanks God for his serene presence as the "more" within one's work—amid tensions, illness, reverses and despite a sometimes profound sense of being empty of God and of being directionless in life. From this one learns trustingly to give up control over one's prayer, work, and associates, and to live vulnerably with them and with one's own limitations.

Scripture demonstrates to the praying person how Christ, precisely in this way, trained his disciples for intimacy with himself and the people by teaching them how to be vulnerable like lambs among the wolves. They learned, too, how to let God into the stretch of their lives, how to find him in life's day-to-day tensions with Pharisees and Sadducees, how to enjoy his presence—despite their rivalries and power-hungers—in the unexpected successes of multiplied loaves and expelled demons. Indeed, they, too, felt the joy of the "more" (Christ) in their work and prayer: they, too, experienced a fresh intimacy with themselves, with God and with his people. What more could they ask for?

6. Sixth Stage: Prayer of Powerlessness

The daring "more" discovered in apostolic prayer opens the generous person to the perils of intimacy whether in marriage (with its incessant companionship, its package-choice of in-laws, and its lottery of children-raising) or in friendship (with its precarious shifts of time-place-life-style, with its demands for follow-through in sickness and disaster, and with its implicit vow of "forever") or in vowed religious life (with its lottery of comrades, its potential for self-satisfied bachelorhood or spinsterhood, its opportunities for sloth and irresponsibility, and its possible Phariseeism of religious profession). Such perils are not the price of intimacy. They are its inevitable occupational hazards in which the prayer of the apostolic "more" stretches the praying person toward fuller intimacy with self, comrades, dependents, and Christ.

Because the three life-styles are perilously complex and demanding, people living them often experience powerlessness, that is, total lack of control over their situation. And this can occur precisely when these people have put in much time and effort and have shared much pain and joy in their community so that they are just beginning to experience rich intimacy and to have high hopes for closer family living, warmer circles of friends and more deeply satisfying religious life. For all these priceless gifts seem to grow daily both in life and in prayer during and despite the haunting call for something more in one's life, during and despite the warring of selfish career-desires with humane desires for sacrifice, during and despite the worries about manipulating God with strategic prayer and sacrifice, during and despite the need for patience with the ambiguities of life—even in the face of death.

Yet the prayer and life of powerlessness is not a hopeless malaise nor an enervating confusion, nor an isolating alienation. Rather, it contains hope, energy, and intimacy since it contains such a trust in others that one no longer tries hard to control them but rather enjoys letting them be independently free and creative. Thus the prayer and life of powerlessness includes a great surrender to God and his providence. This happens to be much more than mere acceptance of a situation beyond one's control.

Fortunately, one is reassured to find in Scripture that the Virgin Mary's life became powerless exactly when she spoke her fiat, that Christ became more powerless as he proceeded from hidden Nazareth to public Jerusalem, that John the Baptist, Paul of Tarsus and the apostles met seeming defeat at the height of their powers. Isaiah's suffering servant (the ideal figure who embodies God's call to Israel) is notably powerless; yet ever since the sixth century B.C., he has attracted women and men to give themselves to God and his people. The beatitudes and woes, used by Christ to describe those who populate his kingdom, also announce that the powerless are

the powerful in Christ's eyes. But, much like St. Peter, each
of us fails to hear this message and strives mightily against
powerlessness all our lives since we dread losing control over
life. Our personal identity seems to be at stake.

For these reasons, Christ gave us the sacrament of
matrimony, his covenant with the marrying couple, to enable
us to risk and to do what pagans claim is impossible: give
mutual loyalty till death. God has offered us the quasi-
sacrament of long-time friendship so that we can discover the
power of lifelong union in the midst of distant separation,
passing time, bitter fights, and fierce suffering. Lastly Christ,
through his Church, has gifted us with vowed religious life,
the quasi-sacrament, which founds something beyond even
friendship: sisterhood and brotherhood in the evangelical life,
strong familial intimacy with God. All three styles of life lead
into the Lord's additional gift (what Ignatius called the second
mode of humility): the conviction that not even in a minor
way would one betray the spouse or the friend or the fellow
vowed religious or God even if the betrayal were to be
rewarded with worldwide power for doing good. Such strong
loyalty provides the solid base from which the apostle can
dare to do frontier work for God's people in their most
pressing needs.

Clearly, this prayer and life of powerlessness is not only a
state of being present with the *anawim* of the beatitudes but
also an attitude of doing whatever one can do for them in
their desperate circumstances. It is not only a constant desire
to let Christ work out through one's weaknesses but also a
willingness to be rewarded with additional powerlessness (a
fuller surrender for deeper intimacy with Christ and with his
people). This gradual surrender of one's autonomy becomes,
then, a fuller revelation of Christ, the "more." For Christian
powerlessness, a life of prudent fear amid strong hope and
trust in one's apostolic work, is the state in which God makes
his presence most powerfully felt in the apostle's weakness
and in the latter's demanding work and prayer.

Here, too, God renders the apostle more tightly united
and more effectively consoling to the helpless people who

need companionship as much as economic aid. For the apostle's powerlessness does not allow him or her as friend, spouse, or vowed religious to control any dependents. But it does enable the apostle to support their liberty so that they are more capable of intimate union with others and with God.

Thus, amid a growing sense of powerlessness, the praying person is nevertheless discovering, reverencing, and promoting God's intimate mediation between spouses, friends, and vowed religious. This prayer, therefore, is an ongoing, humiliating self-revelation of one's need for intimacy and one's inability to achieve or promote it well without God's mediation. For this reason, prayer of powerlessness requires profound trust, readiness to adapt, deep wondering about life's meaning and faithful trusting of God's providence. It is the "more," the Christ, vibrant in one's life precisely because one acknowledges how powerless one's life actually is. It is the great surrender to Christ which then promotes manificent bursts of apostolic energy for his people.

7. Seventh Stage: *Prayer of Being* for Others, Servanthood

The sense of powerlessness in life and prayer strips one down to being-for-others, that is, to intense servanthood. One survives this vocation by way of the *prayer of being*. The latter is paradoxically silent and gestureless yet noisy with distractions, very dry and yet felt as worthwhile, empty of consolations yet deeply satisfying, lacking many former certitudes yet set solid in peace—with only occasional leaps of the heart and with only a rare feeling of God taking over completely in an intense joy. From these characteristics one would be tempted to judge that this prayer denies intimacy. Yet its normal state of passive dryness at the top three levels of human experience reveals by contrast the underlying, majestic presence of the great river of God, the source of all life, at a fourth deepest level. Nor is prayer of being introvertively lonely. Instead it discloses that God and the praying person are beings-for-others in empathy, sensitivity and compassion so that they naturally reach out to serve others.

For Yahweh is so closely identified with his people that he makes them his bride and sends his Son to be incarnately immersed in them and their routinized lives. Indeed, the Son's seven last words of the passion show him sharing his people's destitution and powerlessness. And yet under these seven last words is the strong joy of Christ in doing his Father's will. In this disciplining of Christ, we discover how God disciplines his people so that liberation can occur—a liberation to allow the beloved to grow in independent freedom, to risk everything for the beloved, to learn hunger for God's preferences, and to submit trustfully to the sometime darkness of God's providence. Because of this discipline, God can wonderfully empower the trusting person without any concern that the latter's vanity would abuse the divine powers committed to her or him.

The paradox of this paschal-mystery prayer is that its sweet dryness, full emptiness, teeming desert, light darkness and apparent denial of all intimacy promote a "homing" prayer at the center of the praying person's being. Here one can let God grow freely far beyond one's imprisoning images and concepts of him.

At the same time, one feels strongly drawn to serve others with all one's being, one's being-for-others. In this way one lives more radically the priesthood of the faithful, the sacrament of ordination, and the fierce intimacy of the Ignatian third mode of humility. The latter is the basic attitude of so identifying with the poor and rejected Christ present in his marginal people that one prefers their company to that of others. With these resources one can discern the gentlest apostolic suggestions of the Spirit even when they move one toward excruciating revolutionary decisions. At last we know why we say to the one offering us intimacy: "Go away closer." There is no prayer more demanding, no prayer more apostolically effective, and almost no prayer more intimate.

8. Eighth Stage: Trinitarian Prayer of Ultimate Communion

The persistent joy underlying the Gospel servanthood just described is ultimate communion with self, others, and God. This radical intimacy turns out to be the compenetration of all persons in their very beings. For us it is most clearly symbolized in physical marital intercourse which stands for total psychological compenetration (sharing) of minds and hearts and for the total spiritual compenetration (agreement) of the spouses in their most cherished values, hopes and experiences. Such compenetration of beings, despite all its frustrations, is the beginning of the resurrection since in Christian marriage it leads to compenetration with Christ in the sacraments, with the Spirit in the body of Christ (the Church) and with the Father through Christ and in the Spirit. What is said here of married partners is also true of the perduring faithfulness between friends and in the sisterhood and brotherhood of vowed religious. For each of the three states not only images the Trinity in its life but also promotes the imaging compenetration of personal beings.

This ultimate communion, however, is as humble (and as humorous) as Christ's washing of the apostles' feet, as exalted (and as friendly) as the Last Supper discourse of the evangelist John. This blending of beings is supremely accomplished by the three persons of the Trinity and less wonderously, though remarkably, by all those united in Christ's mystical body, the Church. Toward this union all the sacraments work, but particularly the root-sacrament of the Eucharist. For the latter is the ongoing incarnation of Christ. He is not only the wisdom behind the ongoing creative act within the developing universe but also the constant presence in the sacraments as through them he enters into the peak-events of intimacy in our lives from birth to death.

It is the Holy Spirit, sent by the Father and the Son, who forms the mystical body of Christ through both the sacramental presence and the trinitarian indwelling. For the Holy Spirit breathes Christ into the Eucharist communicated

to each Christian and proclaims within each Christian the
Trinity's presence. As a result, not only are Jesus and the
Trinity compenetratively present in each individual member
of the mystical body, but all members are present in each
other by way of the Eucharistic Christ and the one indwelling
Trinity. To know this and to be able, through the sacraments,
to live this fact fully is to be a Christian and not simply a
believer. It is to image the Trinity explicitly and to reveal it to
all people, however poorly, in one's actions.

Here, too, is found the inner meaning of all liturgical
prayer. For as one moves through the eight steps of growing
presence in the Eucharistic celebration, one recognizes the
various stages of intimacy-prayer: the decisions of individuals
to gather for the Eucharist out of hunger for intimacy, the
actual gathering of the congregation for one-to-one prayer of
intimacy, the confession of sins for forgiveness-intimacy, the
Word heard and homilized for apostolic prayer of the
"more," the gift offering for the prayer of powerlessness, the
consecration for *prayer of being,* and communion for the
ultimate-union prayer of intimacy. Here, step by step, the
stages of prayer of intimacy are revealed and lived.

It should be no surprise, then, that the prayer of ultimate
communion is the finding of Christ's creative act in the
evolving universe, in personal and ecclesial salvation history,
in the new covenant of the sacraments, in the suffering
servant's intense joy at oneness with Christ and his people
(the final intimacy of the great community of the great
tomorrow), and, lastly, in the continual contemplation-to-
attain-divine-love.

All this is a profound contemplation-in-action wherein the
action is totally directed and ultimately vitalized by the
contemplative prayer of passivity. Thus the world is seen as
Christ-centered, as potentially wholesome in peace and
justice, as suffused with the sense of God's affectionate
providence, as revelatory—in its joys and sorrows—of
Christ's joys and sorrows, as developing in the Christian an
always greater capacity for joy. Here is the deepest intimacy
on earth as we move toward absolute intimacy: our entering

into face-to-face Trinity life forever in the communion of saints. This is our total immersion in the Trinity and its joy. Here we find the Father still creating us, the Holy Spirit still befriending us and lifting us out of suffering into eternal joy, and the Christ, Lord of history, still sharing all his personal riches with us. This is the prayer of ultimate communion experienced as second-by-second living forever.

A Last Conclusion

Evidently, these eight stages of intimacy-prayer should not be interpreted rigidly as though the stages were hermetically sealed off from each other or as though the praying person, like some exotic butterfly, left a stage behind when he or she moved to a deeper stage. The first stage, namely, hunger for intimacy, must permeate all stages if they are each to be sought. The second stage, that of daily one-to-one intimacy-prayer, is the root of all types of prayer and, therefore, certainly nourishes the prayers of powerlessness, *being* and ultimate communion. After all, these eight stages or types of intimacy-prayer are basically strong attitudes toward God and others which always remain within the praying person.

On the other hand, these stages of intimacy-prayer are distinct moments of development having diverse signs of intimacy. To deny the distinctness of signs is to foster confusion in the praying person. For if the person does not recognize the new set of signs as a deeper stage of intimacy, he or she may mistakenly estimate that the prayer of intimacy has been lost when actually it is being deepened. Thus it is important to note, for example, that, even though the prayer of powerlessness and the *prayer of being* are commonly marked by dryness and a felt emptiness, nevertheless *prayer of being* has diverse qualities of gestureless silence, of angry fear about backsliding, and of certitudes lost—despite occasional leaps of joy. Thus, too, although the prayer of the apostolic "more" and prayer of powerlessness share a certain absence of God and a powerlessness against opposition, still prayer of powerlessness has the different notes of the haunting call to something more, of the seeming irrelevance of Scripture to one's life, of the interior struggle between professional self-assertion and personal submission to God, and of the patience with life's puzzling ambiguities.

Therefore, one naturally experiences continuity between these types or stages of intimacy-prayer since growing friendship with God is ordinarily continuous. Yet such growth in intimacy demands diverse stages indicating healthy progress. For a human relationship not to grow is for it to deteriorate. Is the prayer-relationship with God not similar?

The descriptions of these eight stages of intimacy-prayer indicate, then, how costly in pain is deep familiarity with self, others, and God. May they also disclose how worthwhile is this dark intimacy which leads so terribly and beautifully into the depths of the self, into the inner life of the *anawim*, into the heart of Christ, and into the ever deepening mystery of God.

Appendix
How the Various Stages of Prayer of Intimacy Relate to the *Spiritual Exercises* of St. Ignatius and to the Chapters of *Radical Prayer*

Stage One: The costly paradox of intimacy discusses the occasions, external manifestations, and conditions for intimacy. The use of these materials may uncover how ready the directee or retreatant is for deeper prayer (what is the hunger for intimacy?) and what type of prayer would be more suited to his or her present needs in beginning direction or retreat.

Stage Two: Day-to-day prayer of intimacy stresses the act of presence before and throughout each prayer-time, faithfulness to daily prayer-times, patience with the slowness of prayer-progress, the sacrament of baptism as root of prayer of daily intimacy, and the Gospel mysteries as the dynamic memories of the risen Christ within the retreatant-directee. See Chapter Three of *Radical Prayer* (Paulist Press, 1984) for the description of the "prayer of Christ's memories."

Stage Three: Prayer of forgiveness demands stark honesty, shows how important are the sacrament of reconciliation and the Scriptures for healing and describes how forgiveness must be continually renewed. See Chapter Two of *Radical Prayer* for the "prayer of reminiscence" as an entrance into the prayer of forgiveness, both of which fit

the first week of the *Spiritual Exercises* of St.
Ignatius.

Stage Four: Prayer of sinfulness sees sin as the rupture of
               intimacy and envisions revelation as God's
               loving act of intimacy toward us to repair this
               rupture beginning in Eden's primal sin and
               progressing through the patriarchs and prophets
               to Christ's advent and the Holy Spirit's coming.
               By way of the sacraments of the sick and of
               reconciliation, one can finally accept the ratty
               and beautiful sides of one's unique personality,
               be astonished at God's patient forgiveness, and
               let God run his world in his own way and time.
               This fits the three Ignatian meditations on sin
               and the aim of the first week. The "prayer of
               listening-waiting" described in Chapter Four of
               Radical Prayer is useful here.

Stage Five: Apostolic prayer of the daring "more" promotes
               realism of working within one's limitations. In
               this way, one discovers how God's presence is
               the "more" in one's work-prayer as one
               stretches the self according to the Ignatian first
               mode of humility. This is how Christ trained his
               disciples to develop intimacy out of the tensions
               of daily vulnerability. Here the kingdom and
               two standard meditations, along with Ignatius'
               meditations on the call and training of the
               apostles, are supported by apostolic prayer of
               the "more." Chapter Five of *Radical Prayer* on
               the "feel of apostolic contemplation-in-action"
               shows the results of the apostolic prayer of the
               "more" as both prayers enrich the second week
               of the *Spiritual Exercises.*

Stage Six: The prayer of powerlessness, within the
               intimacy of marriage, friendship, and vowed

religious life, includes a realistic appraisal of the hazards of these three ways of life. Its Gospel-base demonstrates the need for Ignatian indifference (poised freedom or creative detachment) and for Ignatius' second mode of humility, two pure gifts of God. Along with "prayer of decisioning" found in Chapter Eight of *Radical Prayer* (2nd edition), prayer of powerlessness looks to the Ignatian election as well as to the living out of this decision in the following months.

Stage Seven: *Prayer of being* is filled with the paradoxes of the paschal mystery and the Ignatian third mode of humility. It is a reliving of Christ's passion in all its noisy silence, dry worthwhileness, empty fullness, fearful peace along with its underlying secret joy in the Father's pleasure. It parallels both "prayer of the paschal mystery" of Chapter Nine and "fourth level prayer-experience" of Chapter One in *Radical Prayer* and thus supplements the third week of the *Spiritual Exercises.*

Stage Eight: The prayer of ultimate communion, centered in the Eucharist, deals with the root of intimacy: the compenetration of persons in the Trinity, in the mystical body of Christ, and in marriage-friendship-vowed-religious-life. This compenetration occurs by way of the sacraments and revelation. The Gospel life of the resurrection, the after-life of the great community of the great tomorrow, and the Ignatian contemplation-to-attain-divine-love are all focused in this prayer of ultimate communion. As a result, in *Radical Prayer*, Chapter Seven on "prayer of the secular

Christ" and Chapter Six on "prayer of the indwelling Trinity" are quite relevant.

Overview: In endeavoring to distinguish the eight stages of intimacy and their eight corresponding prayer-types, one can discover a new way to look at the so-called spiritual logic of the *Spiritual Exercises*.

Notes

Preface

1. Katherine M. Dyckman, S.N.J.M. and L. Patrick Carroll, S.J. indicate how the seven sacraments are diverse prayer experiences (especially the Eucharist and reconciliation) wherein one gets to know Jesus in a variety of ways (p. 31). See *Solitude to Sacrament* (Liturgical Press, Collegeville, Minn., 1982).

Stage One

1. I am indebted to James Doyle, S.J. and Carl Dehne, S.J. for their assistance in the writing of this Stage One which Mary Anthony Wagner, O.S.B., editor of *Sisters Today,* kindly published (Vol. 56, 1985/6, pp. 325–330).

2. Henri Nouwen's *The Way of the Heart* (Ballantine, New York, 1981) shows how prayerful solitude strips us of our pretenses, leads us to fuller self-knowledge, and enables us to live humbly in awareness of our sinfulness (pp. 1–16).

3. Because liturgical prayer often induces one-to-one prayer of intimacy, I do not want to deny their mutual influence. I wish to say only that liturgical prayer normally withers without the nourishment of one-to-one prayer of intimacy.

Stage Two

1. Carl Dehne, S.J. and Gerald Gross, S.J. made more accurate this Stage Two which, again, Mary Anthony Wagner, O.S.B. prepublished in *Sisters Today.* (Vol. 57, 1986/8, pp. 451–456).

2. In *Spiritual Passages* (Crossroad, New York, 1984), an intriguing, broadly based synthesis of psychology and spirituality, Benedict J. Groeschel, O.F.M. Cap., demonstrates the crucial importance of intimacy for one's human development and spirituality, using insights from Erikson,

Levenson, and the Whiteheads. Later the lives of outstanding Christians are employed to illuminate the three traditional stages of spiritual development: the purgative, the illuminative, and the unitive.

3. Joseph Martos offers a valuable introduction to *The Catholic Sacraments* (Michael Glazier, Wilmington, Del., 1983) as he outlines a contemporary psychology, sociology, history, and theology of the sacraments before he attempts to describe how the sacraments affect personal, communal, ecclesial, and global spirituality. His insights illuminate each stage of prayerful intimacy as described throughout this present book.

4. Henri Nouwen (*Intimacy*, Harper & Row, San Francisco, 1969) parallels my descriptions of intimacy growth with his stages of religious development (pp. 5–20).

5. In *Christening, the Making of Christians* (Liturgical Press, Collegeville, Minn., 1980) Mark Searle skillfully weaves into the baptismal and confirmational rituals the history, the theology, and the faith-experience demanded of participants. As a result, this is a book to be prayed over.

6. For a much fuller explanation of this "Prayer of Christ's Memories," see Chapter Three of my *Radical Prayer* (Paulist Press, New York, 1984). It is also found in *Sisters Today* (Vol. 49, 1977/2, pp. 74–84).

7. Honesty with self and with God, an honesty based on strong mutual trust, is extolled by Pierre Wolff in *May I Hate God?* (Paulist Press, New York, 1979, esp. pp. 43–56). He also includes, in his Appendix II, a number of scriptural references to angry prayers so that people praying in anger feel less guilt.

8. In his article "Solitude" (*Sojourners*, March 1979) Henri Nouwen distinguishes three types: (1) mere privacy against the community, (2) merely a healing renewal in order better to serve the community, (3) the very grounding of community in God. This latter type of solitude is the source of all personal and group unity so that community can be seen as

a divine gift (not a human fabrication) and so that community living itself becomes unending prayer.

Stage Three

1. Peter Steele, S.J., provincial of the Australian province of the Society of Jesus, gave me some sage advice on this Stage Three. Daniel F.X. Meenan, S.J., editor of *Review for Religious,* not only printed this as an article (Vol. 44, 1985/3, pp. 388–397) but, before doing so, gave incisive critique for improving it notably.

2. Lance Morrow writes with extraordinary sensitivity in the *Time* magazine account (January 9, 1984, p. 33, col. 2) concerning Pope John Paul's forgiveness of Ali Agca, his assassin. He remarks that failure to forgive imprisons one in the past, puts one under the control of the unforgiven person's initiatives, and risks further escalation of the original violence.

3. St. Paul is convinced that the living Gospel is none other than the risen Christ alive within each believer (Rom 1:4, 16; 16:25–27; 1 Cor 15:1–2, 13–14). The printed pages of the Bible, therefore, serve mainly to alert us and to guide us to the risen Christ's dynamic memory of an event or a parable or a teaching as he lives within the reader or the hearer.

4. There is a reciprocal process going on within the triangle of the forgiver, the offender and God. In forgiving my offender, I can begin to forgive myself for my own offenses against others and thus forgive my offender more compassionately. And in forgiving myself and my offender, I can start to forgive God for not doing what I had wanted him to do. In his often wise book, *When Bad Things Happen to Good People* (Avon, New York, 1981) Rabbi Harold Kushner indicates why admitting one's anger at God can be healthy (pp. 107–167). Unfortunately, he strips God of his detailed personal providence in explaining why God is not responsible for our sufferings and tragedies (pp. 129–134, 140–141,

148). Warren W. Wiersbe replies to this in *Why Us? When Bad Things Happen to God's People* (Fleming H. Revell Co., Old Tappan, N.J., 1978).

5. The first three chapters of *As Bread That Is Broken* (Dimension Books, Denville, N.J., 1974, pp. 9–35) by Peter G. van Breemen, S.J. are a powerful appeal for self-acceptance, perhaps the most eloquent appeal of our times.

6. The American epic-films *The Godfather I and II* illustrate how revenge, overwhelming forgiveness, multiplies the "enemy" in ever more violent swirls of hate.

7. In contrasting "the taking form of existence" (the use of sheer power in human relationships) with "the loving form of existence," Henri Nouwen (*Intimacy*, Harper & Row, San Francisco, 1969) reveals how forgiveness (based on the conviction that evil is reversible) arises to make other-centered love possible (pp. 28–37). Incidentally, a second edition of *Intimacy* (Fides Press, Notre Dame, Ind., 1970) includes an additional chapter on "Homosexuality: Prejudice or Mental Illness." This turns out to be an informative, compassionate account of an arrested intimacy-growth.

8. Gustavo Gutiérrez (*We Drink From Our Own Wells*, Orbis, Maryknoll, N.Y., 1984, p. 100) is convinced that to forgive is to choose life and that not to forgive is to choose death. For pardoning opens up possibilities for persons to change, to forge new community, and to initiate a new era for a nation. This is a basic tenet of his liberation spirituality.

9. Within "Prayer of Forgiveness" there is a strong need for "Prayer of Personal Reminiscence" (see my *Radical Prayer*, Paulist Press, New York, 1984, Chapter Two, pp. 20–37). For how will I bring myself to forgive my offender if I do not recognize my own sins against others? How will I have the courage to admit my own sins unless I previously acknowledge the goodness in myself—a goodness I principally owe to those who poured their lives into mine? "Prayer of Personal Reminiscence" is also found in *Review for Religious* (Vol. 36, 1977/2, pp. 213–226).

Stage Four

1. Professional guidance for this Stage Four was received from Peter Steele, S.J. of the University of Melbourne, and from Daniel F.X. Meenan, S.J. Thomas Tobin, S.J. and Mitchell Pacwa, S.J. checked the essay for its scriptural bases and offered numerous stylistic improvements. Kenneth Baker, S.J. graciously accepted it for prepublishing in the *Homiletic and Pastoral Review.* (Vol. 86, 1985/3, pp. 57–66).

2. Robert Harvanek, S.J. in his article "The Reluctance To Admit Sin" (*Studies in the Spirituality of Jesuits,* Vol. 9, 1977/3) maps the shift of balance from a more individualistic understanding of sin (deliberate transgression of a law of God by a responsible person) to a more social concept (corporate sin out of weakness or lack of love for others and for God). He traces the first viewpoint to a human model of unattainable perfection and the second to a growth model of starting where one is in talents, experience, and limitations. Of course, the diverse viewpoints yield different understandings of God (the lawmaker and the healer) and diverse experiences of God in prayer. Reluctance to admit sinfulness is more connected with the first concept of sin than with the second.

3. In his *Problem of Pain* (Macmillan, New York, 1962) C.S. Lewis offers reason for thinking that some animals will be made immortal by God. He feels that they have attained real selves in being tamed (humanized) by their owners and these selves live in the immortality of their human owners since all that exists on the earth is somehow related to man's existence (pp. 138–143).

4. Bernard J. Verkamp in "Recovering a Sense of Sin" (*America,* Nov. 19, 1983, pp. 305–307) relates how the determinists (like Skinner, Hospers, and Lorenz) as well as the literary libertines (like Wilde, Whitman and Norman Brown) have tried to take back all God's personal power and to transfer it to impersonal nature. As a result, the human is encouraged to be subhuman and thus to be free of all guilt. If

this account is accepted, then the sinner could not feel or measure the sinful harm done to others and to the sinner's own self.

5. Hosea (4:1–3) makes clear that human sins destroy all levels of the ecological: "There is no fidelity, no mercy, no knowledge of God in the land. False swearing, lying, murder, stealing and adultery! . . . Therefore, the land mourns and everything that dwells in it languishes: the beasts of the field, the birds of the air, and even the fish of the sea perish."

6. To appreciate the context and the preoccupations of the Pentateuch, one should note *The Vitality of Old Testament Tradition* (John Knox Press, Atlanta, 1975) wherein Walter Brueggemann outlines a history of nineteenth and twentieth century Old Testament studies on the Pentateuch. There he describes the resultant method used by Hans Walter Wolff to discover the kerygma of the four Pentateuch sources. Wolff was convinced that in the text we have four confessions of faith and each has a relation to a particular historical crisis (p. 32).

7. "According to Rahner, Jesus' life, death, and resurrection are not so much a satisfaction for sin as a revelation causing grace and salvation to come about in human history." Thus does Annice Callahan, R.S.C.J. (*Karl Rahner's Spirituality of the Pierced Heart*, University Press of America, Lanham, Md., 1985, p. 62) sum up a basic Rahnerian insight relevant to this Stage Four.

8. For a thorough study of the Trinity's third person seen as "befriending Spirit," consult *Activities of the Holy Spirit* (Herald Franciscan Press, Chicago, 1984) by Edmund Fortman, S.J. who describes the functions of the Holy Spirit as Christic, sanctifying, ecclesial, sacramental, charismatic and personal (pp. 175–183).

9. In *Called by Name* (Dimension Books, Denville, N.J., 1976) Peter G. van Breemen, S.J. distinguishes concrete sins like slandering, cheating, stealing, and so on, from a deeper level of sin which is simply one's careful screening of oneself from God's loving action. At this second level (the cause of all

first-level, concrete sins) a person experiences his or her sinfulness (pp. 75–76).

10. Because "Prayer of Admitted Sinfulness" levels us, it renders us able to listen intently, to confront ourselves gently, to face Christ eye-to-eye, to be patient with the slow coming of the kingdom, to be alert to the changing patterns of our lives, finally to give a reverent trust to others—all manifestations of the "Prayer of Listening-Waiting" which is explored in Chapter Four of my *Radical Prayer* (Paulist, New York, 1984, pp. 51–61) and also found in *Sisters Today* (Vol. 53, 1981/4, pp. 208–215).

11. In *Certain as the Dawn* (Dimension Books, Denville, N.J., 1980) Peter G. van Breemen not only coins the dictum "true mission starts only with remission [of sins]" (p. 64) but also sketches how only God can change the bitter suffering of authentic guilt into joy since one's right reaction to sin and sinfulness is a pure gift from God. Out of this joy at being loved by God in the midst of one's sinfulness comes the drive to become an apostle for Christ and his people (pp. 67–68).

Stage Five

1. The late James Doyle, S.J. along with Robert Thesing, S.J., formerly pastor of Holy Family Church, Chicago, reviewed this Stage Five for me out of their extensive experience of pastoral work.

2. I take the term "super-apostle" from the *New American Bible* (P.J. Kenedy and Sons, New York, 1970) at 2 Corinthians 12:11.

3. Alfred C. Kammer, S.J., along with Richard L. Smith, S.J., Francisco Ornelas, S.J., and Noel Barré, S.J., has delineated the problem of "burnout" among Jesuit social activists without attempting any solutions—though such a description certainly is the first step to the solution—in "'Burn-out'—Contemporary Dilemma for the Jesuit Social Activist" (*Studies in the Spirituality of Jesuits*, Vol. 10, 1978/1).

4. In *Ministry Burnout* (Paulist, New York-Ramsey, 1982) John A. Sanford considers nine factors which contribute to "burnout" (which is not to be confused with exhaustion of the ego, though the two are often correlative). Needless to say, the super-apostle "burnout" is an extreme type which ends up in exhaustion. No one is exempt from "burnout" if one works hard. The problem one faces is: "Can I recognize the oncoming of 'burnout' and learn from experience?"

5. Denis de Rougement remarks in his classic work, *Love in the Western World* (translated by Montgomery Belgion, revised and augmented edition, Princeton University Press, Princeton, N.J., 1983) that the modern mind abhors any deliberate acceptance of a limitation especially in the faithful beloved who is, of course, limited (p. 287). This naturally entails a refusal to recognize one's own inadequacies.

6. *The Road Less Traveled* (Simon and Schuster, New York, 1978) devotes almost a quarter of its length to personal discipline—a rare subject these days. Its author, M. Scott Peck, M.D., defines discipline as a system of basic techniques to deal positively with the pain involved in problem solving (p. 77). These techniques are the delaying of gratification, the assumption of responsibility, the dedication to truth, and the balancing willingness to be flexible in one's responses to problems.

7. The Jesuit Thomas Green's book *When the Well Runs Dry* (Ave Maria Press, Notre Dame, Ind., 1979) graphically depicts increasing dryness in prayer so that the praying person can recognize this experience as a maturing union with God and not as a loss of God's interest in him or her. Chapter Six is particularly illustrative of apostolic prayer of dryness.

8. Such serene and creative prayer is described in Chapter Five of my *Radical Prayer* (Paulist Press, New York, 1984, pp. 62–80): "Prayer of Apostolic Contemplation-in-Action, Welcoming Christ and His World." It is also found in *Review for Religious*, (Vol. 40, 1981/3, pp. 321–337).

9. Gustavo Gutiérrez dramatizes powerfully with "documents of the people" the way interior union with Christ achieves authenticity and drives the apostle to live deeply with his suffering people so that love can effect liberation.

Part III of his *We Drink from Our Own Wells* (translated by
Matthew J. O'Connell, Orbis, Maryknoll, N.Y., 1984) shows
how interior-individual spirituality must be infused with
exterior-social spirituality lest the first be privatized, rendered
individualistic, and even be volatized. He also points out how
the first of the great commandments cannot be lived without
simultaneously living the second of the great commandments.
In this latter one discovers Christ's preference for the poor
and one works toward solidarity with the oppressed by
walking with an entire people according to the Spirit's
guidance. Charity becomes the building of a new Christian
society of free people enjoying the dignity of themselves,
their work, and their worship as they search out God. Thus
Gutiérrez will show little patience with an elitist,
individualistic spirituality which, it is hoped, *Dark Intimacy*
has at least partially escaped.

Stage Six

1. The guidance of Robert Thesing, S.J. and James
Doyle, S.J. was especially helpful in this Stage Six because of
their extensive experience in spiritual direction.

2. The friendship of Jonathan and David was a strong
bond (I Sam 18:3), the Lord's bond (20:8), which was
renewed by oath (20:17) "because he [Jonathan] loved him
[David] as his very self." Indeed, "The Lord shall be between
you and me and between your posterity and mine forever"
(20:42).

3. Paul Hinnebusch, O.P. has described Christian
friendship (*Friendship in the Lord*, Ave Maria Press, Notre
Dame, Ind., 1974) with a rare honesty and depth. In the
second half of the book he shows how crucial friendship is to
prayer.

4. Katherine Dychman, S.N.J.M and L. Patrick Carroll,
S.J. fashion a precise, condensed, and balanced description of
the criteria for recognizing prayer of powerlessness in their
Inviting the Mystic, Supporting the Prophet (Paulist Press, New
York, 1981, pp. 62–68). This issues out of their reflections on
John of the Cross, on Thomas Merton, and on personal
experience in giving spiritual direction.

5. In her book *Waiting for God* (translated by Emma Craufurd, Harper & Row, New York, 1973), Simone Weil's "The Love of God and Affliction" (pp. 117–136) defines such dark ambiguity as *malheur*, remarking that this infinite distance separating the person from God becomes concentrated into one point so that it can pierce the center of one's soul as it did Christ's soul in Gethsemane.

6. Though the infancy narratives hardly enjoy the same historical basis as do Jesus' ministry, death, and resurrection, still these stories carry the Gospel message accurately and richly as Raymond E. Brown has meticulously shown in *The Birth of the Messiah* (Doubleday, Garden City, N.Y., 1977).

7. A realistic contemporary, and yet traditional, portrait of Mary, the mother of God, is drawn by seven scholarly BVM sisters in *Mary According to Women* (edited by Carol Frances Jegen, B.V.M., Leaven Press, Kansas City, Mo., 1985).

8. William F. Kraft's "The Martha Syndrome" (*Review for Religious*, Vol. 43, 1984/3, pp. 430–437) studies with sympathy the plight of those addicted to American workaholism. He suggests ways in which they may rescue themselves from programmed lives and from exhaustion and resultant anger—not by quitting but by reconsidering their basic reasons for becoming religious and by making some simple practical decisions about play and prayer.

9. Lest one think that I have overestimated passivity here and overlooked the active elements of the spiritual life, I call attention to a companion article: "The Prayer of Daily Decisioning: Hungering for God's Will," Chapter Eight of my *Radical Prayer* (Paulist, New York, 1984, softcover edition, pp. 131–157—not in hard cover edition, 1983). This also appeared in *Review for Religious* (Vol. 42, 1983/3, pp. 422–442).

10. In *Sacraments and Sacramentality* (Twenty-Third Publications, Mystic, Conn., 1983) Bernard Cooke calls human love sacramental in the strict sense (p. 86) since sacraments are meant to transform whatever is human by bringing persons under the influence of Jesus' saving action (p. 8) and since friendships include within themselves God's

presence. Though I cannot bring myself to this position, I am indebted to Bernard Cooke for other insights which have influenced the writing of this book.

11. That religious vowed commitment means communal covenant is powerfully delineated by Thomas E. Clarke, S.J. in "Jesuit Commitment—Fraternal Covenant," while John C. Haughey, S.J. in "Another Perspective on Religious Commitment" indicates how the rapid mobility of modern society requires a deepened interior commitment to friend, spouse, and fellow religious. Both articles appear in *Studies in the Spirituality of Jesuits* (Vol. 3, 1971/3).

12. L. Patrick Carroll, S.J. (*To Love, To Share, To Serve: Challenges to a Religious*, Liturgical Press, Collegeville, Minn., 1979) breaks open the traditional explanations of the vows to show new meanings. Poverty becomes open-handed love and open-hearted sharing, chastity turns into the discipline of becoming a celibate lover, and obedience transforms into paying attention to how much God loves me into all I do and into future actions for others.

Stage Seven

1. Fred Bergewisch, S.J. offered extensive style-criticism for this article, while James Doyle, S.J. discovered three passages requiring more accurate expression, thus saving me no little embarrassment. In conversations and letters, Mary Chorda, P.B.V.M., Rita Ryan, R.S.C.J., and M. Trinitas Nordhus, O.S.B. clarified for me what Prayer of Being is.

2. After leading us through the meanings of mental prayer and consequent affective prayer, the masterful Leonard Boase, S.J. offers us in *The Prayer of Faith* (Loyola University Press, 1985, a reprint of Boase's original 1950 text before it was mutilated by "updating") a concretely practical way of recognizing, living with, and even enjoying prayer of dryness which he thinks is John of the Cross' dark night of the senses (pp. 14–16, 40–41, 49–52, 74–77). Perhaps this classic is the best contemporary book available in English for

those troubled by dryness in prayer; it is clear, balanced, and, in its imagery, quietly humorous.

3. This double emptiness, this darkness both inside and outside oneself, is clearly detailed in three progressive steps by Thomas Green, S.J. in *Darkness in the Marketplace* (Ave Maria Press, Notre Dame, Ind., 1981, pp. 74–117).

4. Gerald G. May, M.D., a psychiatrist and also a spiritual director at the Shalem Insititute, Washington, D.C., speaks of this anger against God (pp. 140–141) in his *Will and Spirit* (Harper & Row, New York, 1982). In a daring stand he discovers agapaic (divine) love at the root of narcissistic (self-love), erotic (romantic), and filial (compassionate or caritative) love (pp. 126–171). This agapaic love has divine qualities in its unconditional and permanent aspects (p. 132). Not to understand this is to risk being filled with guilt at one's always conditional love and hence to be angry at God for seemingly demanding divine unconditional love or for seemingly giving only conditional love until one's performance of dutiful deeds is flawless (pp. 139–141).

5. In *Living with Apocalypse* (edited by Tilden H. Edwards, Harper & Row, New York, 1984), Constance FitzGerald, O.C.D. writes "Impasse and the Dark Night" (pp. 93–116) to show how the impasse, the total entrapment of one's life in seeming contradictions, sharp denials, and discouraging limitations, is actually the dark night described by John of the Cross. But she claims that when faced with faith, this night can provide a new vision of one's life, a new energy to live that vision, and a new understanding of who God is. She then applies this interpretation of the dark night socially to the plights of feminists, the American nation, and the Catholic Church. Ernest Larkin, O. Carm. equates Ignatian indifference, biblical faith and John of the Cross' detachment ("The Dark Night," *The Way*, Vol. 14, 1974/1, 13–21) to indicate that John's dark night is simply an explanation of the demands of faith. It is not undergone solely by the saint or mystic; it is the occasional lot of anyone trying to live the Gospel daily.

6. Gerald May, M.D. cautiously offers sharp criteria for distinguishing between depressions, desolations, and dark nights in his *Care of Mind, Care of Spirit* (Harper & Row, New York, 1982, pp. 84–91) and then suggests practical ways for the spiritual director to deal with these diverse phenomena.

7. The whole Chapter One in my *Radical Prayer* (Paulist Press, New York, 1984, pp. 5–19), "The Fourth Level of Prayer Experience: Divining Mystery," explains more fully these four levels of experience and their significance for doing discernment.

8. When Peter G. van Breemen, S.J. (*Called by Name*, Dimension Books, Denville, N.J., 1976, pp. 62–72) wants to discuss the contemplative in action, he describes the prayer experience of this person in terms of *prayer of being*, alert passivity, open-handed generosity, dark union with the Trinity, surrender to intimacy, the blank wall of St. Thérèse of Lisieux's dry emptiness, and inner silence.

9. For Jules Toner, S.J. affective affirmation is radical love because it is the way of actively co-being with the beloved; it unites the acts of being of both beloved and lover—in each other (*The Experience of Love*, Corpus Books, Washington, D.C., 1968, pp. 162–163, 183). Of course, this would account for how *prayer of being* turns a person into being a contemplative in action.

10. C.S. Lewis remarks in his intriguing book *Problem of Pain* (Macmillan, New York, 1967, p. 104) that the real problem is not that some good people suffer but that some evil people do not suffer. Apparently Lewis felt that suffering was so important for people to become humane and wise that God's worst condemnation of a sinner enjoying success from his sins was to give him further success. As a result the latter would continue in evil and so destroy himself and his future.

11. Having already given us *Daily We Touch Him*, a down to earth guide for mental prayer according to the monastic tradition, M. Basil Pennington, O.C.S.O. has capped this with *Centering Prayer* (Doubleday, Garden City, N.Y., 1980), the result of not a few workshops on prayer. It discusses the way of doing centering prayer and its attendant self-acceptance,

distractions, compassion, poverty of spirit, and Scripture reading.

12. Peter G. van Breemen, S.J., in carrying out the basic theme of his books: God's free creative love for us-just-as-we-are, underlines in *Certain as the Dawn* (Dimension Books, Denville, N.J., 1980) how our understanding of God must be continually enlarged (pp. 9–16) as we get to know him better and how this enlargement constantly changes our style of life. In an appendix (pp. 149–152), he contrasts the faith-approach to everyday life with the moralistic approach so that one sees in detail how different are the resultant life-styles and concepts of God.

13. The relevance of John of the Cross' dark night to twentieth century thought and life is sharply limned by Michael J. Buckley, S.J. in his article "Atheism and Contemplation" (*Theological Studies*, Vol. 40, 1979/4, pp. 680–699). He shows how the projection-theories of God elaborated by Feuerbach and Freud to express atheism would be acceptable to John of the Cross. But the latter would correct and supplement these theories with his experience of transformative Christic grace in order to express what contemplation is: the gradual awareness that beyond all illuminating conceptions of God is his dark mystery of infinite being.

14. The *Spiritual Exercises of St. Ignatius* translated by Louis J. Puhl, S.J., Newman Press, 1951, p. 69, # 167.

15. I have sketched this ultimate source for the Ignatian apostolic drive in Chapter Nine of my *Radical Prayer:* "Prayer of the Paschal Mystery: Sorrow in the Risen Lord's Company" (Paulist: New York, 1984, 2nd softcover edition, pp. 158–177; it is not included in the first hardcover edition, 1983). It also appears in an abbreviated form in *Review for Religious* (Vol. 42, 1983/5, pp. 677–690).

Stage Eight

1. Fred Bergewisch, S.J. and James Doyle, S.J. offered me expert advice for this Stage Eight.

2. Paul Quay, S.J. has profoundly explored the symbolism of marriage and virginity at both the natural and scriptural levels in *The Christian Meaning of Human Sexuality* (Credo House, Evanston, Ill., 1985). He brilliantly integrates both sets of symbols to show the beauty and the delicacy of human love.

3. I have recently tried to use a purely philosophical approach to establish how God mediates within our very beings to strengthen all other-centered acquaintanceships, friendships, and loves in *Searching the Limits of Love* (Loyola University Press, Chicago, 1985).

4. A remarkably detailed history of the Christian Church's ever developing doctrine on the Trinity is advanced by Edmund J. Fortman, S.J. in *The Triune God* (Baker Book House, Grand Rapids, Mich., 1982). His concise elaboration of various approaches to the divine indwelling (pp. 303–315) is particularly useful for sounding out this eighth stage of prayerful intimacy. For a quick survey of modern Church documents on the indwelling and for instances of its use in the lives of Teresa of Avila and Sister Elizabeth of the Trinity, see "The Indwelling of the Trinity and St. Teresa's 'Prayer of Recollection'"(*Review for Religious*, Vol. 44, 1985/2, pp. 439–449) by Antonio Moreno, O.P.

5. That this deeper compenetration of being occurs only in a long-term commitment to another and that it enriches all other significant relationships becomes clear in *Should Anyone Say Forever?* (Loyola University Press, Chicago, 1975, pp. 46–54) by John C. Haughey, S.J.

6. The Letters to the Colossians and to the Ephesians stress this compenetrative union of all Christians in Christ (and hence in the Trinity). In Colossians 1:16–20 we find that in Christ all things have been created and continue in being so that he is absolute fullness and reconciles everything in his person. In Colossians 2:9–12 it is clear that each of us has a share in Christ's divine fullness because his resurrection is in us. All this is echoed in Ephesians 1:20–23 and 2:5–6 so that Christ fills all with all (2:21–23; 3:17–19).

7. As Delbert R. Hillers explores *Covenant: The History of a Biblical Idea* (John Hopkins Press, Baltimore, 1973), he reveals how complex is this central theme because of its content and its literary history. He claims against others that for St. Paul there is no clear continuity left between the old covenant of Sinai and the new covenant in Christ (p. 183).

8. Paul Hinnebusch, O.P. in *Friendship in the Lord* (Ave Maria Press, Notre Dame, Ind., 1974, pp. 139–143) displays the risen Christ as holding all things together by his presence in each Church member and as filling the Church with his Holy Spirit, the very power of the resurrection. As a result, the Church is really, not metaphorically, the very body of Christ.

9. Gustavo Gutiérrez (*We Drink from Our Own Wells*, Orbis, Maryknoll, N.Y. 1984, p. 69, and footnote #32) sees the Church as the real body of Christ, an extension of the incarnation; this is not a pretty metaphor but Paul's realism. He approvingly quotes L. Cerfaux (*The Church in the Theology of St. Paul*, Herder and Herder, N.Y., 1959, p. 278) who declares that the Church "is none other than the real and personal body which lived, died, and was glorified, and with which the bread in the Eucharist is identified."

10. This eighth step reveals why thanksgiving after communion is so vital to the praying person's growth. Shortening or omitting such thanksgiving is a retarding of potentially expansive growth.

11. If one is looking for a clear mapping of all the factors which enter into a full Christian life so that it ends up in "ordinary mysticism," then *Response to God's Love* (Loyola University Press, Chicago, 1984) by Edward Carter, S.J. fills that definition.

12. A striking interpretation of this prayer is offered by Michael Buckley, S.J. in "Contemplation To Gain Love" (*The Way*, London, Supplement # 34, 1975, pp. 92–102).

13. In her important recovery of *Karl Rahner's Spirituality of the Pierced Heart* (University Press of America,

Lanham, Md., 1985), Annice Callahan, R.S.C.J. points out
how Rahner sees the soul at death entering into a pancosmic
relationship with all beings. This consummation of the
person's interior life (p. 63) explains the continuing
redemptive influence of Christ's humanity in all graced
human lives (p. 65). She refers then to *The Spiritual Exercises
and the Ignatian Mystical Horizon* (The Institute of Jesuit
Sources, St. Louis, 1976) authored by Harvey D. Egan, S.J.
who sees the humanity of Jesus Christ at the heart of all
reality because of his life, death, and resurrection (pp. 103–
105).

14. See Henri Nouwen's article, "Christ of the Americas"
(*America*, Vol. 150, #1, April 21, 1984, pp. 293–302).

15. There are practical implications when prayer rises out
of this compenetrative union of each Christian with the divine
Trinity. These are outlined in Chapter Six of my *Radical
Prayer* (Paulist Press, New York, 1984, pp. 81–102): "Prayer
of the Indwelling Trinity: Centering in God, Self, and
Others." This also appeared in *Review for Religious* (Vol. 41,
1982/1, pp. 37–52).

16. In the Pentateuch the Lord frequently instructs his
people to set aside a day or week or month for sacrificial
worship and then to make merry during this time (Lev 23:40;
Num 10:10; Deut 12:7–12; 14:22–26; 15:19–20; 16:11–14;
26:11; 27:7; 28:14). Nehemiah remarks that rejoicing in the
Lord is one's strength (8:10). Zechariah sees the fast days as
occasions of joy and gladness, festivals for the people (8:19). 1
Chronicles 30:21–23 reports how, under King Hezekiah
during the Passover, the joyful celebration at the resanctified
temple was extended an extra week.

17. I discuss in some detail the continually expanding
human personality of the risen Christ (which is not to be
confused with his divine act of infinite existence, his divine
personhood) in Chapter Seven of *Radical Prayer* (Paulist, New
York, 1984, pp. 103–130): "Prayer to the Secular Christ—
Risen and Growing Forever."

18. Joseph Awad, "A Creation Canticle," *America*, May 29, 1982, p. 413.

Overview

1. James Doyle, S.J. graciously, as always, offered comments on this Overview, as did Robert Thesing, S.J.